1970

CAESAR'S GALLIC WAR

CAESAR'S GALLIC WAR

Translated by **JOSEPH PEARL**
Formerly Professor and Chairman of
the Department of Classical Languages
BROOKLYN COLLEGE

BARRON'S EDUCATIONAL SERIES, INC.

WOODBURY, NEW YORK

PREFACE

IT IS INDEED a challenge to reproduce in an English translation the directness and simplicity of Caesar's style and at the same time to preserve the spirit and vitality of the original. The task of this translator has been further complicated by his twofold aim. On the one hand, he has endeavored to produce a translation in correct and idiomatic English so that the interest of the general reader may be concentrated upon Caesar's dramatic report of his activities in Gaul over a period of eight years. On the other hand, he has tried to keep his rendition as close to the original as possible so that it may serve as a guidepost and aid to the young student who may be somewhat baffled in his attempt to cope with the original Latin.

LIST OF BIOGRAPHICAL, GEOGRAPHICAL, AND MILITARY TERMS

ACCO. A chief of the Senones, who stirred up his people against the Romans; put to death by Caesar.

AEDUI. A powerful Gallic tribe between the Loire and the Saône.

AGEDINCUM. The chief town of the Senones.

ALESIA. A stronghold of the Mandubii. The siege of Alesia ranks among the decisive military operations of the world.

ALLOBROGES. A powerful Gallic tribe, living between the Rhone, the Isère, Lake Geneva, and the Alps.

AMBIANI. A Belgian tribe, whose chief town, Samarobriva, is now called Amiens.

AMBIORIX. A leader of the Eburones, who destroyed the Roman force under Sabinus and Cotta, and inspired the attack on Cicero's camp.

ANDES. A Gallic people north of the Loire.

ANTONIUS. Marcus Antonius. Mark Antony (born 83, died 30 B.C.), a lieutenant of Caesar in Gaul in 52 and 51 B.C., and afterwards in the Civil War. Member of the Second Triumvirate. Defeated by Octavianus at the battle of Actium. In 30 B.C. committed suicide in Egypt.

AQUILEIA. A city of Cisalpine Gaul.

AQUITANIA.   One of the three main divisions of Gaul
between the Province, the Pyrenees, and the
Garonne.

ARIOVISTUS.   A German king, defeated by Caesar in
58 B.C.

ARVERNI.   A powerful tribe living in the upper part of
the Elaver. Their chief city, Gergovia, was un-
successfully besieged by Caesar.

ATREBATES.   A Belgic tribe living near Arras.

ATUATUCA.   A stronghold in the territory of the Eburones.

ATUATUCI.   A powerful Belgic tribe living on the left
bank of the Meuse.

AULERCI.   A group of tribes living in the interior of
Gaul.

AVARICUM.   The most strongly fortified city of the
Bituriges, besieged and taken by Caesar. Its
inhabitants were put to the sword.

BACULUS.   Publius Sextius Baculus, one of the bravest
of Caesar's centurions.

BALLISTA.   A military engine used for hurling huge
stones or heavy blocks of wood through the air
at an angle of 45°.

BASILUS.   Lucius Minucius Basilus, an officer of Caesar, afterwards one of the conspirators against
him.

BELGAE.   Inhabitants of one of the three main divisions of Gaul.

BELLOVACI.   A powerful Belgic people.

BIBRACTE.   Capital of the Aedui.

BIBRAX.   A town of the Remi, north of the Axona.

BITURIGES.   A tribe in central Gaul.

BOII. A Celtic tribe which migrated westward with the Helvetii.

BRATUSPANTIUM. A fortified town of the Bellovaci.

BRUTUS. Decimus Junius Brutus Albinus. Served under Caesar in the Gallic and Civil Wars; afterwards one of his assassins.

CADURCI. A tribe in Aquitania.

CAESAR. Lucius Julius Caesar, a distant relative of C. Julius Caesar, acting as his legate in 52 B.C.

CAMULOGENUS. A leader of the Aulerci, commander of the Parisii against Labienus.

CANINIUS. Gaius Caninius Rebilus, one of Caesar's lieutenants in the Gallic and Civil Wars.

CANTABRI. A warlike people in the north of Spain.

CARNUTES. A people in Central Gaul. Their chief city was Cenabum.

CASSIVELLAUNUS. Leader of the British army against Caesar in 54 B.C.

CATAPULT. An engine of war used for shooting large arrows or javelins in a horizontal direction.

CATAVOLCUS. A chief of the Eburones. Despairing of success in the war against Caesar, he took poison.

CAVARILLUS. A prince of the Aedui.

CELTILLUS. A prince of the Arverni, father of Vercingetorix.

CENABUM. The chief city of the Carnutes.

CENTURION. An officer risen from the ranks, in charge of a century, consisting of 60 men in Caesar's army.

CHERUSCI. A German tribe north of the Suebi.

CICERO. Quintus Tullius Cicero (brother of M. Tullius Cicero, the orator), one of Caesar's lieutenants in Gaul. He made a heroic defense of his camp in 54 B.C.; was on Pompey's side in the Civil War. Put to death by Antony in 43 B.C.

CINGETORIX. Rival of Indutiomarus, his father-in-law, for the leadership of the Treveri. Loyal to Caesar.

CISALPINE GAUL. Gaul on the Italian side of the Alps.

COHORT. The tenth part of a legion, consisting of 360 men in Caesar's army.

COMMIUS. A leader of the Atrebates and commander in the Gallic army called to relieve Alesia.

CONSUL. One of the two chief magistrates of Rome, chosen annually by the Romans.

CONVICTOLITAVIS. A young Aeduan nobleman, whose claims to the office of Vergobret were sustained by Caesar.

COTTA. Lucius Aurunculeius Cotta, one of Caesar's lieutenants, killed by the Eburones.

CRASSUS. Marcus Licinius Crassus, a member of the First Triumvirate, killed by the Parthians in 53 B.C.

CRASSUS. Marcus Licinius Crassus, elder son of the triumvir. Served as Caesar's *quaestor* in 54 B.C.

CRASSUS. Publius Licinius Crassus, younger son of the triumvir. Served with Caesar as commander of cavalry; was killed by the Parthians in 53 B.C.

CRITOGNATUS. A prominent Arvernian.

DIVICIACUS. A pro-Roman leader of the Aedui, brother of Dumnorix.

DIVICO. A leader of the Helvetii in their war with Cassius, 107 B.C.

DUMNORIX. An anti-Roman leader of the Aedui, brother of Diviciacus, and son-in-law of Orgetorix. While trying to escape from Caesar, he was slain.

EBURONES. A Belgic tribe, living north of the Treveri. For destroying a part of the Roman army under Sabinus and Cotta they were afterwards almost exterminated by Caesar.

EPOREDORIX. A leader of the Aedui, captured by Caesar.

ERATOSTHENES. A Greek scholar of the third century B.C. who was librarian of the great library at Alexandria in Egypt. Famous as a geographer, mathematician, historian, and grammarian.

FABIUS. Gaius Fabius, a lieutenant of Caesar in the Gallic War, and in the first year of the Civil War.

FABIUS. Lucius Fabius, a centurion killed at Gergovia.

GALBA. Servius Sulpicius Galba, one of Caesar's lieutenants in the Gallic War; afterwards one of the conspirators against Caesar.

GALBA. King of the Suessiones.

GERGOVIA. Chief city of the Arverni, in southeastern Gaul, successfully defended by its inhabitants against siege by Caesar.

HARUDES. A German tribe.

HELVETII. A large tribe living between Lake Geneva, the Rhone, and the Rhine.

HELVII. A Gallic people living in the Roman province of Transalpine Gaul.

HERCYNIAN FOREST. A huge forest in southern Germany and Austria, extending from the source of the Danube to the Carpathian Mountains.

ICCIUS. A leader of the Remi.

INDUTIOMARUS. A chief of the Treveri, rival of Cingetorix and hostile to Caesar.

LABIENUS. Titus Labienus, the most prominent of Caesar's lieutenants in the Gallic War. Joined Pompey in the Civil War, and fell at the battle of Munda 45 B.C.

LEGION. The largest unit of the Roman army, consisting of 3600 men in Caesar's army.

LEMOVICES. A Gallic tribe west of the Arverni.

LEXOVII. A tribe of northwestern Gaul.

LIEUTENANT. An officer, in command of one or more legions, next in rank to the commander-in-chief.

LINGONES. A Gallic tribe west of the Sequani.

LISCUS. A chief magistrate (Vergobret) of the Aedui.

LITAVICCUS. A prominent Aeduan.

LUCTERIUS. A leader of the Cadurci and an assistant to Vercingetorix in the great revolt of 52 B.C.

LUTETIA. A city of the Parisii on an island in the Seine. The Latin name for Paris.

MANDUBII. A Gallic tribe north of the Aedui. Their chief city was Alesia.

MANDUBRACIUS. A British chief, loyal to Caesar.

MANIPLE. One-third of a cohort, consisting of 120 men in Caesar's army.

MARIUS. Gaius Marius, a great Roman general, conquered the Cimbri and Teutones in 101 B.C. Seven times consul; champion of the popular party.

MELDI. A Gallic tribe between the Seine and the Marne.

MENAPII. A Belgic tribe near the mouth of the Rhine.

METLOSEDUM. A town of the Senones, on an island in the Seine.

MILITARY TRIBUNE. One of six staff officers attached to each legion.

MORINI. A Belgic tribe, living on the seacoast opposite Kent.

NANTUATES. A Gallic tribe living southeast of Lake Geneva.

NARBO. Capital of the Province.

NERVII. A powerful Belgic tribe.

NITIOBROGES. A tribe in Northern Aquitania.

NOREIA. Chief city of the Norici.

NOVIODUNUM. Name of three different towns:
1. A town of the Aedui, on the right bank of the Loire.
2. A town of the Bituriges, near Cenabum.
3. A town of the Suessiones, on the Aisne.

OCELUM. A town of the Graioceli in the Alps.

OCTODURUS. Chief town of the Veragri, situated in the Rhone valley southeast of Geneva.

ORGETORIX. A Helvetian nobleman who formed a plot to seize the supreme power.

OSISMI. A coast tribe of northwestern Gaul.

PARISII. A Gallic tribe on the Seine, on the site of Paris.

PEDIUS. Quintus Pedius, a nephew of Caesar and a lieutenant under him in Gaul. Consul in 43 B.C.

PICTONES. A Gallic people south of the Loire.

PISO. Lucius Calpurnius Piso, a lieutenant in the army of Cassius which was defeated by the Helvetii in 107 B.C.

PISO. Lucius Calpurnius Piso Caesoninus, father of Calpurnia, Caesar's wife. Consul in 58 B.C.

PISO. A brave Aquitanian.

PLANCUS. Lucius Munatius Plancus, a lieutenant in Caesar's army.

POMPEIUS. Gaius Pompeius Magnus, Caesar's son-in-law and rival, defeated by Caesar at the battle of Pharsalus, and afterwards murdered in Egypt.

POMPEIUS. Gnaeus Pompeius, an interpreter of Quintus Titurius Sabinus.

PORTUS ITIUS. Harbor from which Caesar sailed to Britain, probably Boulogne.

QUAESTOR. Quartermaster in charge of the military chest, the pay, food, and clothing of the soldiers. Sometimes placed in command of a legion.

REGINUS. Gaius Antistius Reginus, a lieutenant of Caesar.

REMI. A powerful Belgic tribe on the Aisne.

RUTENI. A Gallic people, west of the Cebenna Mountains, some of whom lived in the Roman Province..

SABINUS. Quintus Titurius Sabinus, a lieutenant of Caesar, killed in an ambuscade prepared by Ambiorix.

SANTONES or SANTONI. A Gallic people on the seacoast.

SCORPION. A military engine; a small catapult.

SEDUNI. A people in the Alps, southeast of Lake Geneva.

SEMPRONIUS. Marcus Sempronius Rutilus. A Roman cavalry officer.

SENONES. A Gallic people south of the Marne, whose chief city was Agedincum.

SEQUANI. A Gallic people west of the Jura Mountains, whose chief city was Vesontio.

SEXTIUS. Titus Sextius, a lieutenant of Caesar.

SILANUS. Marcus Silanus, a lieutenant of Caesar.

SOTIATES. A people of Aquitania.

SUEBI. A powerful German people.

SUESSIONES. A Belgic people north of the Marne.

SUGAMBRI. A German tribe.

SULPICIUS. Publius Sulpicius Rufus, a lieutenant of Caesar in Gaul and in the Civil War.

TASGETIUS. A prince of the Carnutes.

TENCTERI. A German people, driven from their country by the Suebi.

TESTUDO. A movable shed to protect the soldiers near the enemy's wall. Also a covering formed by the shields of the soldiers held above their heads.

TRANSALPINE GAUL. Gaul beyond the Alps.

TREBONIUS. Gaius Trebonius, a lieutenant of Caesar in the Gallic and Civil Wars; afterwards one of the conspirators against Caesar.

TREBONIUS. Gaius Trebonius, a Roman knight serving in Gaul.

TREVERI. A Belgic people near the Rhine.

UBII. A German tribe living on the Rhine.

USIPETES. A German tribe on the lower Rhine.

VATINIUS. Publius Vatinius, one of Caesar's officers.

VELLAUNODUNUM. A town of the Senones.

VENELLI. A tribe on the northwestern coast of Gaul.

VENETI. A sea-faring Gallic people, on the west coast.

VERAGRI. A Gallic people on the upper Rhone.

VERCASSIVELLAUNUS. One of the four generals in command of the Gallic army raised for the relief of Alesia.

VERCINGETORIX. An Arvernian commander-in-chief of the Gallic forces in 52 B.C.

VERTICO. A Nervian of rank, employed by Cicero during the siege of the camp.

VINEA. A shed built of heavy timbers covered with hides. Several *vineae* placed end to end enabled attacking forces to approach the enemy's wall in safety.

VIRIDOMARUS. A nobleman of the Aedui.

VIRIDOVIX. A leader of the Venelli.

VIROMANDUI. A Belgic tribe near the Remi.

VOLUSENUS. Gaius Volusenus Quadratus, a military tribune.

CONTENTS

BOOK IV

BOOK V

BOOK VI

BOOK VII

CAESAR IS CONSIDERED by many "the greatest Roman of them all." He was a peerless leader of his soldiers; a distinguished man of letters; a forceful and convincing orator, second only to Cicero, who is rated as the greatest Roman orator; and the foremost statesman of his day. Simplicity is the keynote of all of Caesar's activities.

BOOK I

CHAPTER 1

ALL GAUL is divided into three parts, one of which is inhabited by the Belgae, another by the Aquitani, a third by those who in their own language are called Celtae, in our own, Galli. All these differ from one another in language, institutions, and laws. The Galli are separated from the Aquitani by the river Garonne, from the Belgae by the Marne and the Seine. Of all these peoples the bravest are the Belgae, because they are farthest removed from the civilization and refinement of the Roman Province and are very rarely visited by traders who bring in those wares which tend to make people effeminate; and also because they are nearest to the Germans, who live across the Rhine, with whom they are continually at war. For this reason the Helvetii also surpass the rest of the Gauls in valor, because they engage in almost daily skirmishes with the Germans, either trying to keep them out of their own territory, or themselves carrying on war in German territory. One part of these territories which, as has been said, the Gauls occupy, begins at the river Rhone; it is bounded by the Garonne river, the Ocean, and the territory of the Belgae; on the side of the Sequani and the Helvetii it touches the river Rhine; it lies to the north. The country of the Belgae begins at the far boundary of Gaul and extends to the lower part of the river Rhine; it lies to the northeast. Aquitania extends from the Garonne river to the Pyrenees mountains and that part of the Ocean which is near Spain; it lies to the northwest.

CHAPTER 2

AMONG THE HELVETII, by far the noblest and richest man was Orgetorix. In the consulship of Marcus Messala and Marcus Piso, this man, led on by a desire for royal power, formed a conspiracy with the nobles and persuaded the citizens to go out of their territory with all their possessions, saying that, since they excelled all in valor, it was exceedingly easy to secure the sovereignty of all Gaul. To this course he persuaded them the more easily because the Helvetii are hemmed in on all sides by natural features: on one side by the Rhine, a very wide and deep river, which separates the Helvetian territory from the Germans; on a second side by the exceedingly high Jura range, which lies between the Sequani and the Helvetii; on a third side by Lake Geneva and the river Rhone, which separates our Province from the Helvetii. Because of these conditions it came about that they were more restricted in their movements and could less easily make war on their neighbors; and on that account, as they were men fond of waging war, they were greatly distressed. Moreover, considering their population and their reputation for war and bravery, they felt that they had too small a territory, which extended two hundred and forty miles in length and one hundred and eighty in width.

CHAPTER 3

PROMPTED BY these considerations and stirred to action by the influence of Orgetorix, they determined to make ready such things as were necessary for emigration, to buy up the largest possible number of draft animals and carts, to sow as much grain as possible so as to have an adequate supply of grain on the march, and to establish peace and friendship with the neighboring states. They thought that two years would be sufficient to complete these preparations. By law they fixed their departure for the third year. To carry out these arrangements Orgetorix was chosen. He took upon himself the office of envoy to the states. In the course of his journey, he persuaded the Sequanian Casticus, whose father, Catamantaloedes, had held the chief authority among the Sequani for many years and had been called "Friend" by the Senate of the Roman people, to seize in his own state the sovereignty which his father had held before him. He also persuaded the Aeduan Dumnorix, brother of Diviciacus, who at that time held the foremost place in his state and was very popular with the masses, to make a similar attempt, and gave him his daughter in marriage. He convinced them that it was very easy to carry through their undertakings because he himself was going to seize the sovereign power in his own state; there was no doubt that the Helvetii were the most powerful people in all Gaul; he assured them that he would get kingships for them with his own resources and his armed retinue. Won over by this argument, they exchanged an oath-bound pledge of good faith; they hoped that, when they had seized the supreme power, they would be able with the help of three most powerful and very firmly established peoples to become masters of the whole of Gaul.

CHAPTER 4

THIS INTRIGUE WAS REPORTED to the Helvetii by informers. In accordance with their custom, they compelled Orgetorix to plead his case in chains. If condemned, the penalty of being burned alive would inevitably follow. On the day appointed for the pleading of the case, Orgetorix gathered from every quarter to the trial all his slaves, about ten thousand men, and he brought to the same place all his retainers and debtors, of whom he had a large number; with their help he evaded the pleading of his case. When the state, aroused by this, tried to enforce its right by arms, and the public officials brought together a large body of men from the country, Orgetorix died; and there is ground for suspecting, as the Helvetii think, that he committed suicide.

CHAPTER 5

AFTER HIS DEATH the Helvetii tried nevertheless to abide by their decision to leave their territory. As soon as they thought that they were prepared for this undertaking, they set fire to all their fortified towns, about twelve in number, their villages, about four hundred, and the rest of their private buildings;

they burned all their grain except that which they were going to carry with them, so that, by taking away the hope of returning home, they might be the readier to meet any dangers. They ordered every man to bring with him from home a supply of flour for three months. They persuaded their neighbors, the Rauraci, the Tulingi, and the Latobrigi, to adopt the same plan, to burn their fortified towns and villages, and to set out with them; and they received and associated with themselves as allies the Boii, who had lived across the Rhine, but had crossed over into the territory of the Norici and had attacked Noreia.

CHAPTER 6

THERE WERE ONLY TWO ROUTES by which they could leave home. One led through the territory of the Sequani; it was narrow and difficult, between the Jura range and the river Rhone, where carts could hardly be drawn along one at a time; moreover, a very high mountain overhung, so that very few men could easily stop them. The other route led through the Roman Province; it was much easier and more convenient, because between the territory of the Helvetii and the Allobroges, who had recently been subdued, flows the Rhone, and this is in some places fordable. The most remote town of the Allobroges and the nearest to the territory of the Helvetii is Geneva. From this town a bridge extends to the Helvetii. They believed that they either would persuade the Allobroges, because they did not yet seem kindly disposed toward the Roman people, or would compel them by force to al-

low them to go through their territory. When all preparations had been completed for their departure, they
set a day on which they were all to assemble on the
bank of the Rhone. This day was the fifth before the
Calends of April, in the consulship of Lucius Piso
and Aulus Gabinius.

CHAPTER 7

WHEN IT HAD BEEN REPORTED to Cae-
sar that the Helvetii were trying to march through the
Roman Province, he hastened to leave Rome, rushed
with the utmost possible speed to Transalpine Gaul,
and came to the vicinity of Geneva. He levied upon the
entire Province the greatest possible number of soldiers
(there was only one legion in Transalpine Gaul); he
ordered the bridge which was near Geneva to be destroyed. When the Helvetii were informed of his arrival, they sent as envoys to him the most distinguished
men of the state (this delegation was headed by Nam-
meius and Verucloetius) to say that it was their intention to march through the Province, without any mischief, because they had no other route; that they
requested that they might be allowed to do this with
his consent. Because Caesar remembered that the consul Lucius Cassius had been slain and his army routed
by the Helvetii and sent under the yoke, he did not
think that their request ought to be granted. He did
not believe that men of hostile temper, if given an opportunity of marching through the Province, would refrain from violence and mischief. However, in order
that a period might intervene until the soldiers he had

levied should assemble, he replied to the envoys that he would take time for consideration; if they wished anything, they should return on the ides of April.

CHAPTER 8

MEANWHILE, WITH THE AID of the legion which he had with him and the soldiers who had assembled from the Province, he constructed a rampart, sixteen feet high, and a trench, from Lake Geneva, which flows into the river Rhone, to the Jura range, which separates the territory of the Sequani from the Helvetii, a distance of nineteen miles. When this work had been finished, he stationed pickets at intervals and strongly fortified redoubts so that he could stop them more easily if they tried to cross without his permission. When the day which he had appointed with the envoys came, and they returned to him, he said that, following the custom and precedent of the Roman people, he could not grant anyone a right of way through the Province, and he made it clear that, if they tried to use force, he would stop them. Disappointed in their expectations, some of the Helvetii joined boats together and made a number of rafts; others, fording the Rhone where the depth of the river was least, tried, sometimes by day, more often by night, to see whether they could break through. But they were forced back by the strength of the fortifications, the rapid massing of our soldiers, and a shower of weapons, and they gave up the attempt.

CHAPTER 9

THERE WAS LEFT only the route through the territory of the Sequani, by which, because of the narrowness, they could not march without the permission of the Sequani. Since they could not by their own influence persuade these, they sent envoys to the Aeduan Dumnorix in order to gain their request from the Sequani through his intercession. Dumnorix had very great influence among the Sequani because of his popularity and generosity, and he was friendly toward the Helvetii, because from that state he had married the daughter of Orgetorix. Led on by his desire for royal power, he was anxious for a revolution, and he wished to have as many states as possible placed under obligation to himself. Therefore he undertook the mission, and prevailed upon the Sequani to allow the Helvetii to pass through their territory. He also brought about an exchange of hostages between them: the Sequani gave hostages not to prevent the Helvetii from their march; the Helvetii undertook to pass through without mischief and violence.

CHAPTER 10

WORD WAS BROUGHT BACK to Caesar that the Helvetii intended to march through the land of the Sequani and that of the Aedui into the territory of the Santones, which is not far from the borders of the Tolosates, a state which is in the Roman Province. He realized that if this were to take place, it would be

a source of great danger to the Province to have warlike men, unfriendly to the Roman people, as neighbors to a district which was unprotected and very fertile. For these reasons he placed the lieutenant Titus
Labienus in command of the fortification which he had
constructed; he himself hurried into Cisalpine Gaul by
forced marches; there he enrolled two legions, and
brought out of their winter quarters three that were
wintering about Aquileia; and with these five legions
he hastened to march to Transalpine Gaul by the nearest route across the Alps. There the Ceutrones, the
Graioceli, and the Caturiges seized commanding
heights and tried to stop the march of his army. Driving them off in a number of engagements, Caesar
marched from Ocelum, the last town of Cisalpine Gaul,
and on the seventh day reached the territory of the
Vocontii in Transalpine Gaul; from there he led his
army into the territory of the Allobroges, and from the
Allobroges into the territory of the Segusiavi. These
are the first tribe outside the Province, across the
Rhine.

CHAPTER 11

BY THIS TIME the Helvetii had led their
troops through the narrow pass and the territory of the
Sequani, had arrived in the territory of the Aedui, and
were laying waste their fields. Since the Aedui were
unable to defend themselves and their possessions from
them, they sent envoys to Caesar to ask for help. These
pleaded that the Aedui had at all times deserved so
well of the Roman people that their fields ought not to

be laid waste, their children ought not to be led away into slavery, their towns ought not to be taken by assault, almost in sight of the Roman army. At the same time the Ambarri, relatives and kinsmen of the Aedui, informed Caesar that their fields had been laid waste and that they could not easily keep the force of the enemy from their towns. Likewise the Allobroges, who had villages and possessions across the Rhone, fled to Caesar and stated that they had nothing left but the bare ground. Influenced by these events, Caesar decided not to wait until the Helvetii should destroy all the possessions of the allies and move into the territory of the Santoni.

CHAPTER 12

THERE IS A RIVER called the Arar, which flows through the territories of the Aedui and the Sequani into the Rhone—a river of incredible sluggishness, so that with the naked eye it cannot be determined in which direction it flows. This river the Helvetii were crossing by rafts and boats joined together. When Caesar was informed by scouts that the Helvetii had already led three-quarters of their troops across that river, and that almost a quarter was left on this side of the Arar, he set out from camp in the third watch with three legions and came to that division which had not yet crossed the river. Attacking them when they were hampered by baggage and off their guard, he killed a great number of them; the remainder took to flight and hid in the nearest woods. This canton was called Tigurinus; the entire Helvetian state is divided into four cantons. This was the only canton which had left its country, and within the memory of our fathers had killed the consul Lucius Cassius and had sent his army under the yoke. And so, whether by chance or by the design of the immortal gods, that section of the Helvetian state which had brought a notable disaster upon the Roman people was the first to pay the penalty. And in this case Caesar avenged not only public wrongs but also his private wrong, for in the same battle in which the Tigurini had killed Cassius, they had also killed the lieutenant Lucius Piso, the grandfather of Lucius Piso, Caesar's father-in-law.

CHAPTER 13

AFTER THIS BATTLE, in order to be able to pursue the rest of the Helvetian forces, Caesar had a bridge built over the Arar and led his army across. Alarmed at his unexpected arrival, for they saw that he had accomplished the crossing of the river in a single day, a feat which they themselves had accomplished with the greatest difficulty in twenty days, they sent ambassadors to him. The leader of the embassy was Divico, who had been the commander of the Helvetii in the war with Cassius. He treated with Caesar as follows: If the Roman people would make peace with the Helvetii, they would go to and stay in that place where Caesar would decide and wish them to be. But if he continued to make war upon them, he should remember the previous disaster of the Roman people and the old-time valor of the Helvetii. As to the fact that he had attacked one canton unawares, when those who had crossed the river were unable to bear assistance to their comrades, he ought not on that account presume overmuch of his own valor or despise them. They had learned from their fathers and ancestors to fight with courage rather than to rely upon deceit or stratagem. Therefore he should not allow that place where they would make a stand to take its name from a disaster of the Roman people and the annihilation of a Roman army, or to transmit the memory of that disaster to posterity.

CHAPTER 14

CAESAR REPLIED, as follows, that for this reason he had less hesitation, because he remembered those events which the Helvetian ambassadors had mentioned; and he felt all the more indignant because they had happened not at all in accordance with what the Roman people deserved. If the Romans had been conscious of having done any wrong, it would not have been difficult to take precautions; but they had been misled, because they did not understand that they had done anything which should cause them to fear, and they thought that they ought not to be afraid without cause. And even if he were willing to forget an old wrong, could he also erase the memory of their fresh outrages—that against his will they had tried to march through the Province by force, that they had molested the Aedui, the Ambarri, and the Allobroges? The fact that they were boasting so arrogantly of their victory, and the fact that they marveled that they had so long perpetrated wrongs without punishment pointed to the same conclusion. For the immortal gods were wont to grant for a time a more prosperous estate and a more prolonged impunity to those whom they wished to punish for their wickedness in order that they might suffer more bitterly in consequence of a reverse of fortune. Yet, in spite of all this, if he were given hostages by them so that he might feel confident that they would perform their promises, and if they made restitution to the Aedui and the Allobroges for the outrages inflicted on them and their allies, he would make peace with them. Divico replied that the Helvetii had inherited such traditions from their ancestors that they were accustomed to receive, not to give, hostages; of that fact the Roman people were witness. After making this reply he departed.

CHAPTER 15

NEXT DAY THE HELVETII moved their camp from that spot. Caesar did likewise, and sent ahead the whole of his cavalry, four thousand in number, which he had collected from the entire Province, from the Aedui and from their allies, to see in what direction the enemy were marching. Pursuing the enemy's rear too eagerly, our cavalry joined battle with the cavalry of the Helvetii on unfavorable ground, and a few of our men were killed. Elated by this battle, because with five hundred of their cavalry they had routed so large a body of the Roman cavalry, the Helvetii began sometimes to halt with greater boldness and to harass our men with their rear guard. Caesar kept his men from battle and considered it sufficient for the present to prevent the enemy from pillaging, foraging, and laying waste the country. In this way they marched for about fifteen days, so that no more than five or six miles intervened between the enemy's rear and our van.

CHAPTER 16

MEANWHILE EVERY DAY Caesar kept asking the Aedui for the grain which they had promised in the name of the state. For on account of the cold weather not only were the grain-crops unripe in the fields, but there was not even a sufficient supply of fodder at hand. Moreover, he was unable to use the supply of grain which he had brought up the river Arar in boats, because the Helvetii had diverted their march from the river, and he did not wish to lose contact with them. The Aedui put him off from day to day; they kept saying that the grain was being collected, that it was being brought in, and that it was just at hand. When he realized that he was being put off too long, and that the day was approaching when he would have to distribute grain to the soldiers, he summoned the leading men of the Aedui, of whom he had a great number in his camp. Among them were Diviciacus and Liscus, the latter of whom was their highest magistrate, whom the Aedui call Vergobret. This magistrate is elected annually, and has the power of life and death over his countrymen. He took them severely to task because he received no help from them at so critical a time, with the enemy so close, when grain could neither be bought nor taken from the fields, especially since, influenced in great measure by their entreaties, he had under-

taken the campaign; he complained all the more bitterly because he had been abandoned.

CHAPTER 17

THEN AT LENGTH LISCUS, induced by
Caesar's remarks, revealed what till then he had kept
secret. There were some individuals whose influence
with the common people carried very great weight,
who as private citizens had more power than the magistrates themselves. These persons, by seditious and
shameless talk, were holding back the people from
furnishing the grain which they were under obligation
to furnish; they said that, if the Aedui could no longer
maintain the supremacy in Gaul, it was better to endure the rule of Gauls rather than that of Romans;
and they ought not to doubt that if the Romans conquered the Helvetii, they would take away the liberty
from the Aedui as well as from the rest of Gaul. These
were the men by whom our plans and whatever is going on in the camp were reported to the enemy; these
could not be restrained by him. Moreover, in revealing
this pressing matter under compulsion to Caesar, he
realized with how great risk he had acted, and for that
reason he had kept silent as long as he could.

CHAPTER 18

CAESAR REALIZED that by these remarks
of Liscus, Dumnorix, the brother of Diviciacus, was
meant; but as he did not want these matters discussed
in the presence of so many persons, he quickly dis-

missed the assembly, but detained Liscus. He questioned him in private about what he had said at the meeting. Liscus spoke more freely and boldly. Caesar questioned others privately upon the same matters, and he found that Liscus' statements were true: That in fact it was Dumnorix to whom Liscus had referred, a man of the utmost audacity, of strong influence among the common people because of his generosity, and eager for a revolution. For many years he had farmed the tolls and all the other taxes of the Aedui at a low price, because when he bid no one dared bid against him. By these means he had increased his private fortune and had amassed great resources for bribery. At his own expense he always maintained a large body of cavalry and kept it about his person; he had great influence not only in his own state, but also in the neighboring states. To increase his influence, he had given his mother in marriage to the noblest and most powerful man among the Bituriges; he himself had chosen a wife from among the Helvetii; his half-sister on his mother's side and other female relatives he had settled in marriage among other states. Because of his marriage, he favored and wished success to the Helvetii, and personally he hated Caesar and the Romans, because on their arrival his own influence had been lessened, and his brother, Diviciacus, had been restored to his former position of influence and honor. If anything should happen to the Romans, he entertained the highest hope of securing the kingship with the help of the Helvetii; but under the supremacy of the Roman people he despaired not only of the kingship but also of that influence which he now possessed. In the course of questioning, Caesar also discovered that, in the disas-

trous cavalry engagement which had taken place a few
days before, the beginning of that flight had been made
by Dumnorix and his cavalry (for Dumnorix was in
command of the cavalry which the Aedui had sent as
an aid to Caesar) and that because of their flight the
rest of the cavalry had been thrown into a panic.

CHAPTER 19

CAESAR FOUND OUT all these things; besides, other undeniable facts were added to these
grounds of suspicion. It was Dumnorix who had led
the Helvetii through the territory of the Sequani and
who had arranged an exchange of hostages between
them. He had done all this not only without Caesar's
authorization and that of the state, but even without
their knowledge; and he was now accused by the magistrate of the Aedui. Caesar therefore felt that there
was sufficient reason why he should either punish him
himself or order the state to do so. One consideration,
however, weighed against all these things—namely,
his knowledge that Diviciacus, the brother of Dumnorix, showed the utmost devotion to the Roman people
and the utmost affection toward Caesar himself. Caesar was also familiar with his remarkable loyalty, his
fairness, and his self-control; he was afraid that by pun-
ishing Dumnorix he might offend Diviciacus. Therefore, before taking further steps, he ordered Diviciacus
to be summoned to his quarters; he dismissed the ordinary interpreters, and conferred with him through
Gaius Valerius Pracillus, a leading man in the Province of Gaul, an intimate friend of his, in whom he had

the utmost confidence in all matters. He called to mind what had been said in his presence at the assembly of the Gauls, and disclosed what each man had told him separately. He besought and urged Diviciacus that without offense to his feelings Caesar might either hear the case himself and pass judgment upon him, or order the state of the Aedui to do so.

CHAPTER 20

BURSTING INTO TEARS, Diviciacus embraced Caesar, and entreated him not to deal too severely with his brother. He said that he knew that the reports were true, and no one suffered more because of it than he. For while he himself enjoyed the greatest influence in his own state and in the rest of Gaul and Dumnorix very little because of his youth, it was through his help that his brother had risen in power. Dumnorix had used the resources and strength that Diviciacus helped him acquire not only to lessen his brother's popularity, but almost to destroy him. Nevertheless, he was influenced by affection for his brother and by public opinion. For if too severe a fate should befall Dumnorix at the hands of Caesar, while he himself held so high a place in Caesar's friendship, no one would believe that it was done without his consent; because of this the feelings of all Gaul would turn from him. While with tears in his eyes he pleaded with Caesar at great length, Caesar grasped his right hand; reassuring him, he asked him to put an end to his pleading. He declared that his influence with him was so great that in response to his wishes and his prayers he would disregard both the injury to the Roman state and his own resentment. He summoned Dumnorix to his quarters, and he had his brother present; he pointed out what he had against him; he set forth what he himself knew and what the Aedui complained of; he warned him to avoid all grounds of suspicion for the future, and said that he would forgive the past for the sake of his brother, Diviciacus. He placed watches over Dumnorix so that he might know what he did and with whom he spoke.

CHAPTER 21

ON THE SAME DAY he was informed by scouts that the enemy had encamped at the foot of a mountain eight miles from his own camp, and he sent men to find out what were the natural features of the mountain and what the ascent was like from the opposite side. Word was brought back that it was easy. At the third watch Caesar ordered Titus Labienus, his second-in-command, to ascend the highest ridge of the mountain with two legions and with those who had reconnoitered the route as guides; he showed him what his plan was. At the fourth watch Caesar himself hastened toward the enemy along the same route which they had taken, and he sent forward all his cavalry. Publius Considius, who was considered very experienced in the art of war, who had served in the army of Lucius Sulla and afterwards in that of Marcus Crassus, was sent ahead with the scouts.

CHAPTER 22

AT DAWN, when the top of the mountain was occupied by Labienus, and Caesar himself was no more than a mile and a half from the enemy's camp, and, as he afterwards learned from prisoners, neither his own approach nor that of Labienus had been discovered, Considius with his horse at full speed dashed up and reported that the mountain which he had wished to be seized by Labienus was in the possession of the enemy; he said that he had found this out from the Gallic arms and the crests of their helmets. Caesar led his troops up the nearest hill and drew up a line of battle. Labienus had been ordered by Caesar not to join battle unless his own troops were seen near the enemy's camp, so that an attack might be made simultaneously from all sides upon the enemy. Having seized the mountain, he waited for our men and refrained from giving battle. Finally, late in the day Caesar learned through his scouts that the mountain was held by his own troops and that the Helvetii had moved their camp and that Considius, thoroughly frightened, had reported as seen what he had not seen. On that day he followed the enemy at the usual interval, and pitched his camp three miles from their camp.

CHAPTER 23

THE NEXT DAY, as only two days remained before grain would have to be distributed to the army, and as Caesar was not more than eighteen miles from Bibracte, by far the largest and wealthiest town of the Aedui, he decided that he must provide for his grain supply; he turned his line of march away from the Helvetii and set out hastily for Bibracte. This new movement was reported to the enemy by runaway slaves of Lucius Aemilius, a decurion of the Gallic cavalry. The Helvetii thought that the Romans were moving away from them because they were panic-stricken, the more so because on the day before they had not joined battle after seizing a higher position; or they may have been confident that the Romans could be cut off from their grain supply. Whatever the reason, they too changed their plans, reversed their course, and began to pursue and harass our men in the rear.

CHAPTER 24

AFTER CAESAR NOTICED THIS, he withdrew his forces to the nearest hill and sent his cavalry to check the enemy's attack. Meanwhile, halfway up the hill he himself drew up a triple line of his four veteran legions; he ordered the two legions which he had recently levied in Cisalpine Gaul and all the auxiliary troops to be posted on top of the hill, and its entire upper part to be filled with men. He also ordered the packs to be collected in one spot, and that spot to be guarded by those who had taken up their position in the upper line. The Helvetii followed with all their carts and collected their baggage in one place; by a very close formation they hurled back our cavalry, and in a compact mass they moved up against our front line.

CHAPTER 25

CAESAR REMOVED first his own horse and then the horses of all the mounted officers in order to equalize the danger of all and take away the hope of flight. Then he encouraged his men and joined battle. Hurling their javelins from their higher position, our soldiers easily broke up the mass formation of the enemy. Having thrown them into disorder, they drew their swords and made an attack upon them. The Gauls were at a great disadvantage in the fight because several of their shields were often pierced and pinned together by the blow of a single pike; and, as the iron had become bent, they could neither pull it out nor fight to advantage with their left arms hampered, so that many, having jerked their arms back and forth for a long time, preferred to drop the shields from their hands and to fight with their bodies unprotected. At length, worn out with wounds, they began to fall back, and as there was a height nearby about a mile away, they began to retreat there. They reached the hill; and as our men followed them, the Boii and Tulingi, who with about fifteen thousand men brought up the rear of the enemy and formed the rear guard, directly after marching attacked our men on the right flank, and began to move around them. Noticing this, the Helvetii, who had retreated to the hill, began to press forward again and to renew the battle. The Romans changed front and advanced in two divisions, the first and second lines to oppose those who had been defeated and driven back, the third to check the fresh assault.

BOOK 23

CHAPTER 26

THUS THE BATTLE RAGED fiercely for a long time on two fronts. When they could no longer withstand the attacks of our men, the Helvetii retreated to the hill, as they had begun previously, while the Boii and Tulingi retired to their baggage and wagons. For throughout this entire battle, although the fighting lasted from the seventh hour until evening, no one could see the enemy turned to flight. Even at the baggage the fighting continued until late at night, for they had made a rampart of their carts, and from their superior position they kept hurling their javelins at our advancing men, and some of them from between the wagons and wheels kept wounding our men by throwing spears and darts from below. After a long fight, our men gained possession of the baggage and the camp. There the daughter of Orgetorix and one of his sons were captured. About a hundred and thirty thousand of the enemy survived this battle, and marched without pause all through that night; the march was not interrupted for any part of the night, and they arrived in the territory of the Lingones on the fourth day. Our men were unable to pursue them because of the wounds of the soldiers and the burial of the dead. Caesar sent letters and messages to the Lingones, ordering them not to aid the Helvetii with grain or anything else; if they gave such assistance, he would consider them in the same light as the Helvetii. After an interval of three days, he began to follow them with all his forces.

CHAPTER 27

COMPELLED BY THE LACK of supplies, the Helvetii sent envoys to Caesar to treat of surrender. These met him on the march, threw themselves at his feet, and, addressing him in suppliant fashion, with tears begged for peace. Caesar ordered them to await his arrival in the place where they were, and they obeyed. When Caesar arrived at that place, he demanded hostages, arms, and the slaves who had fled to them. While these were being sought for and brought together, about six thousand men of the canton called Verbigenus, either struck by fear that they might be punished after giving up their arms, or prompted by the hope of safety, because they supposed that in so vast a crowd of prisoners their own flight either could be kept hidden or might entirely remain unnoticed, at nightfall left the Helvetian camp and hastened toward the Rhine and the German frontier.

CHAPTER 28

NOW WHEN CAESAR found this out, he commanded those through whose territories they had marched to seek them out and to bring them back, if they wished to be free from guilt in his sight; after they had been brought back, he treated them as enemies; all the rest were allowed to surrender after they had delivered the hostages, their arms, and the deserters. He ordered the Helvetii, the Tulingi, and the Latobrigi to return to their territories from which they had come.

Since all the produce of the fields was gone and they had nothing in their own country with which to relieve their hunger, he directed the Allobroges to give them a supply of grain; he ordered the Helvetii themselves to restore the towns and villages which they had burned. This he did especially for the following reason. He was unwilling that the district from which the Helvetii had departed should remain unoccupied, lest the Germans, who dwell across the Rhine, should, on account of the good quality of the fields, cross from their own territories into those of the Helvetii and so become neighbors of the Province of Gaul and of the Allobroges. He granted the request of the Aedui that they might allow the Boii, known to be men of remarkable courage, to settle in their territories. The Aedui gave them lands and afterwards admitted them to the same state of rights and freedom as they themselves enjoyed.

CHAPTER 29

IN THE CAMP of the Helvetii, tablets were found, written in Greek characters, and they were brought to Caesar. In these an account had been drawn up listing by name the number of those who had gone out from their home and were capable of bearing arms, and likewise listing separately the numbers of children, old men, and women. The aggregate was 263,000 Helvetii, 36,000 Tulingi, 14,000 Latobrigi, 23,000 Rauraci, and 32,000 Boii. Of these who could bear arms there were approximately 92,000. The grand total was about 368,000. Of those who returned home, after a census was taken in accordance with Caesar's command, the number was found to be 110,000.

CHAPTER 30

UPON THE CONCLUSION of the war with the Helvetii, ambassadors, consisting of the leading men of almost all the states of Gaul, came to congratulate Caesar. They said that they understood that, although in the war he had exacted punishment on the Helvetii for the old wrongs they had done to the Roman people, yet that event was just as advantageous to Gaul as to the Roman people. For the Helvetii had left their homes, though their circumstances were exceedingly prosperous, with the design of making war upon the whole of Gaul and of becoming its masters. Out of a great number of localities they intended to select for their abode the spot which they judged to be the most convenient and the most fertile of all Gaul, and to hold the rest of the states as tributaries. The ambassadors asked that with Caesar's permission they might be allowed to call a meeting of all Gaul for a given day; they had, they said, certain matters which in accordance with a general understanding they wished to ask of him. This request was granted; they appointed a day for the assembly, and mutually bound themselves by an oath that no one should make known the proceedings except those to whom the task should have been assigned by general consent.

CHAPTER **31**

WHEN THIS ASSEMBLY had been dismissed, the same leading men who had been with Caesar before returned and asked that they might be allowed to confer with him privately, in a secret place, concerning their welfare and that of the whole country. When their request had been granted, in tears they all threw themselves at Caesar's feet, declaring that they were just as anxious to prevent the disclosure of what they might say as they were to gain their request; for they saw that if disclosure should be made, they would be put to the greatest torture. The Aeduan Diviciacus spoke in their behalf. "In all Gaul," he said, "there are two factions; the Aedui hold the headship of one of these, the Arverni that of the other. When these had struggled fiercely with each other for supremacy for many years, it came about that the Germans were brought over for pay by the Arverni and the Sequani. At first, about fifteen thousand of them had crossed the Rhine; then, when these savage and uncouth barbarians had formed an eager desire for the land, the civilization, and the wealth of the Gauls, more were brought over; now there are about a hundred and twenty thousand of them in Gaul. With these the Aedui and their dependents have fought time and again; but they were defeated and suffered great disaster; they lost all their men of rank, their entire senate, and all their knights. Crushed by these battles and disasters, although previously they had been very powerful in Gaul both because of their own bravery and because of the ties of hospitality and friendship

with the Roman people, they were compelled to give
to the Sequani the noblest men of the state as hostages, and to bind the state by an oath that they would
not try to get back the hostages, nor solicit the aid of
the Roman people, nor refuse to be forever under the
sway and sovereignty of the Sequani. I am the only
one of the entire Aeduan state who could not be prevailed upon to take the oath or to give my children as
hostages. For that reason I fled from my country and
went to the Senate at Rome to ask for aid, because I
alone was bound neither by an oath nor by hostages.
But a worse fate has befallen the victorious Sequani
than the vanquished Aedui. For Ariovistus, the king of
the Germans, settled in their territory, and seized a
third part of the Sequanian territory, which was the
best in the whole of Gaul, and is now ordering them
to withdraw from another third, because a few months
before twenty-four thousand Harudes came to him, for
whom homes and settlements had to be provided. Thus
it will come about that within a few years all the Gauls
will be driven from their territory, and all the Germans
will cross the Rhine; for the territory of Gaul must not
be compared with that of Germany, nor must the
standard of living of the Gauls be compared with that
of the Germans. Moreover, after Ariovistus defeated
the forces of the Gauls in a battle which took place at
Admagetobriga, he began to exercise an arrogant and
cruel tyranny, demanding as hostages the children of
every man of rank, inflicting upon them all kinds of
punishment and tortures if anything was not done at
his nod or pleasure. He is a savage, quick-tempered,
and reckless man; it is impossible to endure his tyranny any longer. Unless they receive some help from

Caesar and the Roman people, all the Gauls will have
to do as the Helvetians have done—emigrate from their
country, seek another dwelling-place, other settlements
far from the Germans, and endure whatever fortune
may befall them. If these words of mine should be disclosed to Ariovistus, I do not doubt that he will inflict
the most severe punishment on all the hostages who
are in his power. You, Caesar, by your own influence
and that of your army, or by your recent victory, or
by the very name of the Roman people could prevent
a larger number of Germans from being brought
across the Rhine, and defend the whole of Gaul from
the outrages of Ariovistus."

CHAPTER 32

WHEN DIVICIACUS had delivered this
speech, all who were present began with loud weeping
to beg Caesar for help. He noticed that of all the company the Sequani alone did not act like the rest, but,
with bowed heads, gazed disconsolately on the ground.
Caesar was surprised, and asked them the reason for
their behavior. The Sequani, however, made no reply,
but silently continued in the same state of dejection.
When he questioned them again and again and could
not elicit a word from them, the same Diviciacus the
Aeduan spoke as follows: "On this account the lot of
the Sequani is more wretched and grievous than that
of the rest, because they alone do not dare even in secret to complain or to beg for aid. They dread the
cruelty of Ariovistus in his absence, just as if he were
present in person, because the rest at any rate have a

chance of escape, but the Sequani, who had admitted Ariovistus within their territories, and whose towns are all in his power, have to endure all possible tortures."

CHAPTER 33

WHEN HE HAD LEARNED THIS, Caesar comforted the Gauls with reassuring words and promised that this matter would have his attention; he had great hopes that Ariovistus, induced by his kindness and his authority, would put a stop to his outrages. After delivering this speech, he dismissed the assembly. And besides those considerations, many reasons induced him to think that he ought to face this problem and take proper action. First of all, he saw that the Aedui, who had been repeatedly called "Brothers" and "Kinsmen" by the Senate, were held in a state of slavery and subjection to the Germans, and he was aware that their hostages were in the hands of Ariovistus and of the Sequani, a state of affairs which in view of the greatness of the power of the Roman people he considered exceedingly disgraceful to himself and to the state. Moreover, if the Germans should gradually become accustomed to cross the Rhine and if large numbers of them should come into Gaul, he realized that this practice would be dangerous for the Roman people. He did not suppose that wild and savage men, after seizing all of Gaul, would refrain from passing over into the Province and pushing on from there into Italy, as the Cimbri and Teutoni had done before them, especially as only the Rhone separated the Sequani from the Roman Province. He therefore thought that he ought to act at the earliest possible moment. As for Ariovistus himself, he had assumed such insolent airs, such arrogance that he seemed unbearable.

CHAPTER 34

CAESAR THEREFORE RESOLVED to send envoys to Ariovistus to demand of him that he choose some spot midway between them for a conference. He wished, he said, to discuss with him matters of state and affairs of the utmost importance to both. To these envoys Ariovistus replied that if he himself had wanted anything from Caesar, he would have come to him; if Caesar wanted anything of him, he ought to come to him. Furthermore, he did not dare come without an army into those parts of Gaul which Caesar was occupying, and he could not, without a great store of supplies and much trouble, bring his army together into one place. Moreover, he could not understand what business either Caesar or the Roman people might have in his Gaul which he had conquered in war.

CHAPTER 35

WHEN THIS REPLY had been brought back, Caesar sent envoys again to him with this message: Although Ariovistus had been treated with such great kindness by himself and the Roman people (for it was in Caesar's consulship that he had been called "King and Friend" by the Senate), he showed this

gratitude to Caesar and to the Roman people, that
when invited to a conference, he raised objections, and
did not consider himself under obligation to discuss
and take under advisement a matter of mutual interest. Therefore Caesar made the following demands of
him: first, that he should not bring any more large
bodies of men across the Rhine into Gaul; secondly,
that he should restore the hostages he held from the
Aedui, and that he should grant the Sequani permission to restore to the Aedui the hostages held by them;
finally, that he should not harass the Aedui, nor make
war upon them and their allies. If he submitted to his
demands, Caesar and the Roman people would maintain a lasting kindly feeling and friendship toward
him. But if Caesar did not obtain his wish, inasmuch
as in the consulship of Marcus Messala and Marcus
Piso the Senate had decreed that the governor of the
Province of Gaul should, as far as he could do so consistently with the public interest, protect the Aedui and
the other friends of the Roman people, he would not
overlook the wrongs suffered by the Aedui.

CHAPTER 36

TO THIS MESSAGE Ariovistus replied as
follows: It was the right of war that those who had
conquered should govern in whatever way they pleased
those whom they had conquered. The Roman people
were accustomed to govern those they had conquered
not according to the dictates of another, but according
to their own judgment. If he himself did not dictate
to the Roman people in what way they should exercise

their right, he ought not to be hindered by the Roman
people in the enjoyment of his own right. Inasmuch as
the Aedui had tried the fortune of war, had contended
in arms, and had been conquered, they had become subject to the payment of tribute. Caesar was doing him a
great injury, for by his arrival he was making his
revenue less profitable to him. He would not restore
the hostages to the Aedui, nor would he make war on
them or their allies without just cause, if they should
abide by the terms that had been agreed upon, and
paid their tribute yearly; if they did not do this, the
title of "Brethren of the Roman people" would be far
from benefiting them. As for Caesar's warning to him
that he would not overlook the wrongs suffered by the
Aedui, no one had ever fought with Ariovistus without his own destruction. Let him come on when he
pleased; he would learn what the invincible Germans,
most thoroughly trained in arms, who for fourteen
years had not been beneath a roof, could accomplish by
their valor.

CHAPTER 37

AT THE TIME when this message was
delivered to Caesar, envoys came from the Aedui and
the Treveri. The Aedui came to complain that the Harudes, who had lately been brought over into Gaul,
were laying waste their territory, and that not even by
giving hostages had they been able to purchase peace
from Ariovistus. The Treveri reported that one hundred cantons of the Suebi had halted on the banks of
the Rhine, and were attempting to cross this river; that

the brothers Nasua and Cimberius were in command
of them. Greatly disturbed by this news, Caesar
thought that he ought to make haste, lest, if a new
band of the Suebi should unite with the old forces of
Ariovistus, it might be more difficult to resist them.
Therefore as quickly as possible he arranged for a supply of grain and hastened by forced marches to meet
Ariovistus.

CHAPTER 38

WHEN HE HAD ADVANCED a three days'
march, it was reported to him that Ariovistus was hastening with all his forces to seize Vesontio, the largest
town of the Sequani, and had advanced a three days'
march from his own territory. Caesar thought that he
ought to take every precaution to prevent the seizure of
this town. For there was in that town the greatest
abundance of all things which were useful for war, and
it was so strongly fortified by natural features that it
afforded excellent opportunity for prolonging the war.
The river Dubis, as though drawn around by a pair of
compasses, almost encircles the whole town; the remaining space, not more than six hundred feet wide,
where the river breaks off, is closed in by a mountain
of great height, in such a way that the banks of the
river touch the base of the mountain on either side. A
wall built around the mountain converts it into a citadel, and joins it with the town. Caesar hastened there
by forced marches by night and by day, and seizing
the town, stationed a garrison in it.

CHAPTER **39**

WHILE HE WAS DELAYING a few days near Vesontio in order to secure grain and other supplies, in consequence of the questioning of our men and the stories of the Gauls and traders, who declared that the Germans were men of huge size, of incredible valor and practiced skill in arms (they said that often meeting the Germans they could not even look them in the face and endure the keenness of their eyes), suddenly so great a panic seized the whole army that it affected in no slight degree the minds and hearts of all. This panic first started with the military tribunes, the subsidiary officials, and the others, who had followed Caesar from Rome from motives of friendship, but had no great experience in warfare. Each one of these, offering a different excuse which he said made it imperative for him to leave, begged Caesar's permission to depart with his consent. Some, influenced by a sense of shame, remained in order to avoid the suspicion of cowardice. These could neither control their features, nor at times restrain their tears; hiding in their tents, they either bewailed their fate, or together with their intimate friends deplored the common danger. Generally throughout the camp wills were being made. Because of the remarks and fear of these, gradually even those who had great experience in the army, soldiers and centurions, and those who were in command of the cavalry, were greatly disturbed. Those of them who wished to be considered less cowardly declared that they were not afraid of the enemy, but feared the narrow roads and the vast forests which lay between them and Ariovistus, or that the grain supply could not be brought up readily enough. Some even told Caesar that when he gave the order to strike camp and advance, the soldiers would not obey the command, and because of their fear would not move forward.

CHAPTER 40

WHEN CAESAR HEARD THIS, he called a council and summoned to it the centurions of all the companies. He severely reprimanded them, in the first place because they presumed to suppose that it was their business to inquire or consider in what direction or with what purpose they were being led. He said that Ariovistus had, in his own consulship, most eagerly sought the friendship of the Roman people; why should anyone suppose that he would so recklessly evade his obligation? He at least was convinced that after his demands had been made known and the fairness of the terms had been clearly understood, Ariovistus would not reject the offer of his goodwill and that of the Roman people. But if, carried away by rage and madness, he should make war, what, after all, were they afraid of? Why would they despair either of their own valor or of his careful leadership? Trial had been made of that enemy in the time of our fathers, when, on the defeat of the Cimbri and Teutoni by Gaius Marius, the army clearly earned no less praise than the commander himself. Trial had also recently been made in Italy, at the time of the uprising of the slaves, notwithstanding the fact that the experience and training which they had gained from us aided them to some extent. From this one may judge how great an advantage there is in steadfast courage, for the very men whom for a long time our men had feared without cause when they were without arms, these they vanquished afterwards, though they were equipped with arms and had won victories. Finally, these were the same Germans with whom the Helvetii had frequent encounters, and whom they had generally defeated not only in their own territory, but also in the territory of the Germans; and yet the Helvetii had been unable to be a match for our army. If the defeat and the flight of the Gauls alarmed any of the soldiers, these, upon inquiry, might discover that, when the Gauls had become exhausted by the length of the war, Ariovistus, who had kept himself secluded for many months within his camp and in the marshes, and had given them no chance to attack him, fell upon them suddenly when, despairing of a battle, they had scattered at last, and conquered them more by cunning and strategy than by valor. Even Ariovistus himself could not expect that our armies would be caught by such strategy for which there had been a chance against inexperienced natives. Those persons who assigned their fear to a pretended anxiety about supplies and the difficulties of the road, acted presumptuously, as they seemed to despair of their general's sense of duty or else to direct him what to do. These matters were his own concern. The Sequani, the Leuci, and the Lingones were supplying grain, and the grain crops in the fields were already ripe; as for the road, within a short time they would be able to judge for themselves. As for the statement that the soldiers would not obey orders or advance, he was not at all disturbed at that;

for he knew that in the case of any commanders whose
armies proved mutinous either their luck had failed
them in consequence of the bad handling of some undertaking, or else some crime of theirs had been discovered, and avarice had been clearly proved against
them. His own integrity had been clearly seen during
his entire life, his good fortune in the war with the
Helvetii. Therefore he would at once do what he had
intended to put off to a more distant day, and he would
break camp the next night, in the fourth watch, in order that he might find out as soon as possible whether
honor and duty or fear had stronger influence with
them. Even if no one else would follow, he would nevertheless march with the Tenth Legion alone, about
which he entertained no doubts, and it would be his
bodyguard. Caesar had greatly favored this legion, and
had the fullest confidence in it because of its valor.

CHAPTER 41

AFTER THIS ADDRESS, the feelings of all
were changed in a remarkable way, and the utmost enthusiasm and eagerness for prosecuting the war arose;
through their military tribunes the soldiers of the
Tenth Legion were the first to express thanks to him
for having expressed a most favorable opinion of
them, and assured him that they were quite ready to
carry on the war. Then the rest of the legions arranged
with their military tribunes and the centurions of the
first rank to apologize to Caesar; they said that they
had never felt either doubt or fear, and realized that
the determination of the general plan of campaign was

not their business but that of the commander. Caesar
accepted their apology. With the help of Diviciacus,
whom Caesar trusted more than any other Gaul, he discovered a route by which he could lead the army
through open country, by a detour of more than fifty
miles. He then set out in the fourth watch, as he had
said he would. On the seventh day of continous marching he was informed by his scouts that the forces of
Ariovistus were twenty-four miles from ours.

CHAPTER 42

WHEN HE LEARNED of Caesar's arrival,
Ariovistus sent ambassadors to him to say that with
regard to the conference Caesar had previously demanded, so far as Ariovistus was concerned, it might
now take place, because Caesar had come nearer, and
he was of the opinion that he could do it without risk.
Caesar did not reject the proposal; he thought that
Ariovistus was at length returning to his senses, inasmuch as on his own initiative he offered what he had
previously refused; and he had great hopes that in return for the great benefits conferred upon him by Caesar and the Roman people, he would desist from his
obstinate course when he learned Caesar's demands.
The fifth day after that was fixed for the conference.
Meanwhile, while ambassadors were being sent back
and forth between them, Ariovistus demanded that
Caesar should not bring any infantry to the conference.
He said that he was afraid that he might be treacherously surrounded by Caesar; he proposed that each
of them should come accompanied by cavalry; he

would not come under any other condition. Because Caesar did not wish the conference to be broken off by a pretext, and because he did not dare to entrust his safety to the cavalry of the Gauls, he decided that it was most expedient to take away all the horses from the Gallic cavalry and to mount upon them the legionary soldiers of the Tenth Legion, in which he had absolute confidence, so that he might have a bodyguard as friendly as possible if there should be any need of action. While this was being done, one of the soldiers of the Tenth Legion remarked, not without wit, that Caesar was doing more than he had promised; he had promised to consider the Tenth Legion as his bodyguard, but now he was enrolling them as Knights.

CHAPTER 43

THERE WAS A LARGE PLAIN, and on it a mound of earth of considerable size. This place was about equally distant from the camps of Ariovistus and Caesar. To this place, as agreed, they came for the conference. Caesar stationed the legion which he had brought on horseback two hundred paces from this mound. Likewise, the cavalry of Ariovistus halted at an equal distance. Ariovistus demanded that they should confer on horseback, and that they should bring with them to the conference ten men each. When they arrived at the spot, at the beginning of his speech Caesar recalled the favors he and the Senate had conferred upon Ariovistus; he reminded him that he had been called "King" and "Friend" by the Senate, and that magnificent presents had been sent to him. He pointed out that this distinction had fallen to the lot of but few, and was usually granted in return for great services; although Ariovistus had no right of approach to the Senate and no just ground for claiming anything, he had obtained these distinctions by the kindness and generosity of Caesar and the Senate. He then stated how old and how just were the reasons for the close relationship between the Romans and the Aedui; what decrees of the Senate, how many and how complimentary, had been passed in their behalf; how at all times the Aedui had held the supremacy of all Gaul, even before they had sought the friendship of Rome. It was the policy of the Roman people to desire that its allies and friends should not only lose none of their possessions, but should grow richer in influence, prestige, and distinction; who then could allow that what they had when they became friends of the Roman people should be taken from them? He then made the same demands as those which he had given to the envoys in his instructions: that Ariovistus should not make war either upon the Aedui or their allies; that he should restore their hostages; and if he could not send back home any part of the Germans, at any rate he should not allow any more to cross the Rhine.

CHAPTER 44

ARIOVISTUS REPLIED briefly to the demands of Caesar, but he had much to say about his own merits. He had crossed the Rhine not of his own accord, but upon the request and summons of the Gauls; he had left home and relatives not without great hope of rich rewards; he had settlements in Gaul ceded by the Gauls themselves; the hostages had been given with the consent of the Gauls themselves; by the rights of war he took tribute which conquerors were accustomed to impose upon the conquered. He had not made war upon the Gauls, but the Gauls upon him; all the states of Gaul had come to attack him, and had set up camp against him; all these forces had been beaten and overcome by him in a single battle; if they wished to try again, he was prepared to fight it out again; but if they wished to enjoy peace, it was unfair to refuse to pay the tribute, which of their own free will they had paid up to that time. The friendship of the Roman people ought to be a distinction and a protection to him, not a loss; and he had sought it with that hope. If through the interference of the Roman people the tribute should be discontinued and the prisoners of war should be taken from his control, he would renounce the friendship of the Roman people as gladly as he had sought it. As to his bringing over a large number of Germans into Gaul, he was doing this in order to protect himself, not to attack Gaul; the proof of this was that he had not come without being asked, and that he had not made war, but had acted on the defensive. He had come to Gaul before the Roman people. Never before this time had an army of the Roman people gone outside the boundary of the Province of Gaul. What did Caesar mean? Why did he come into his territory? This part of Gaul was his province, just as the other was Roman. As no concession ought to be made to him, if he made an attack on Roman territory, so, likewise, we had no right to interfere with him in the exercise of his rights. As to Caesar's saying that the Aedui were called "Brethren" by the Senate, he was not such a fool, nor so unversed in affairs as not to know that neither in the last war with the Allobroges had the Aedui rendered assistance to the Romans, nor in the struggles which the Aedui had with him and the Sequani had they enjoyed the assistance of the Roman people. He had good reason to suspect that Caesar, under the guise of friendship, had an army in Gaul for the purpose of crushing him. Unless Caesar departed and withdrew his army from these parts, he would regard him not as a friend, but as an enemy. Moreover, if he should kill Caesar, he would do a kindness to many nobles and leading men of the Roman people (he had found this out from them through their agents) and he could purchase the favor and friendship of all of these by Caesar's death. On the other hand, if Caesar departed and handed over to Ariovistus the possession of Gaul without interference, he would compensate him with a great reward, and whatever wars Caesar might wish carried on he would finish without any trouble or risk on the part of Caesar.

CHAPTER 45

CAESAR SPOKE AT LENGTH to show why he could not give up the plan he had formed: Neither his own principles nor those of the Roman people would allow him to abandon allies who had deserved so well, and he did not feel that Gaul belonged to Ariovistus any more than to the Roman people. The Arverni and the Ruteni had been subdued in war by Quintus Fabius Maximus, but the Roman people had pardoned them, had not reduced them to a province, and had not imposed a tribute. If priority of time was to be considered, then the sovereignty of the Roman people in Gaul was absolutely right; if the decision of the Senate was to be regarded, then Gaul ought to be free, for, although it had been conquered, the Senate had wished that it should enjoy its own laws.

CHAPTER 46

WHILE THESE MATTERS were being discussed in the conference, it was reported to Caesar that the cavalry of Ariovistus was approaching nearer the mound, riding up to our men, and throwing stones and javelins at them. Caesar stopped speaking, withdrew to his men, and commanded them not to discharge any missile at all against the enemy. For although he saw that an engagement with the cavalry would involve no danger to his chosen legion, still he thought that, if the enemy were routed, he ought not to give anyone the chance of saying that under the guise of a pledge of good faith they had been surrounded by him during the conference. As soon as it was reported to the rank and file with what arrogance at the conference Ariovistus had denied to the Romans all right to be in Gaul, how his cavalry had made an attack upon our men, and how this action had broken off the conference, the soldiers were inspired with a much greater enthusiasm and eagerness for battle.

CHAPTER 47

TWO DAYS LATER, Ariovistus sent envoys to Caesar. He desired, he said, to discuss with him those matters which they had begun to discuss, but had not settled. Caesar was asked either to appoint another day for a conference, or, if he did not wish to do so, to send to him one of his officers. There did not appear to Caesar any good reason for a conference, especially as on the previous day the Germans could not be restrained from hurling missiles at our men. He thought that it would be very dangerous to send one of his officers to Ariovistus and to expose him to savage men. It seemed best to send to him Gaius Valerius Procillus, the son of Gaius Valerius Caburus, a young man of the greatest courage and refinement, whose father had been presented with citizenship by Gaius Valerius Flaccus. He selected him both for his fidelity and for his knowledge of the Gallic tongue, which Ariovistus, from long practice, now spoke fluently, and because in his case the Germans had no reason for offering violence; and with him he sent Marcus Metius, who enjoyed the friendship of Ariovistus. He instructed them to learn what Ariovistus had to say and to report back to him. When Ariovistus saw them before him in his camp, he called out loudly in the presence of his army: Why had they come to him? Was it in order to act as spies? When they tried to speak, he stopped them, and threw them into chains.

CHAPTER 48

THE SAME DAY Ariovistus moved his camp and halted at the foot of a mountain six miles from Caesar's camp. The next day he led his forces past Caesar's camp, and pitched camp two miles beyond him, with the intention of cutting off Caesar from the grain and supplies that were being brought up from the Sequani and the Aedui. For five days in succession Caesar brought his forces out in front of the camp, and kept them drawn up in line of battle, so that if Ariovistus wished to engage in battle, he might not lack the opportunity. All this time Ariovistus kept his army within the camp, but engaged daily in cavalry skirmishes. The method of fighting in which the Germans had trained themselves was as follows: There were six thousand horsemen, and as many foot soldiers, very swift and brave men, whom the horsemen had chosen from the entire force, each one selecting a foot soldier for his personal protection; the horsemen associated themselves with these in battle. To them they would retire; if there was an unusually serious difficulty, the foot soldiers would rush to the rescue; if a horseman was severely wounded and fell from his horse, the foot soldiers would gather round him; if it was necessary to advance in any direction unusually far, or to retreat more rapidly, so great was their speed acquired by training, that holding onto the manes of the horses, they kept pace with them.

CHAPTER 49

WHEN CAESAR SAW that Ariovistus kept himself in camp, in order that he might not be cut off from supplies any longer, he chose a suitable spot for a camp beyond that place in which the Germans had encamped, about six hundred paces from them; having drawn up his army in triple line formation, he proceeded to that place. He ordered the first and second lines to remain under arms, the third to fortify the camp. This spot, as has been said, was about six hundred paces from the enemy. To this place Ariovistus sent about sixteen thousand light-armed men with all the cavalry, in order that these forces might frighten our men and prevent them from proceeding with the work. Nevertheless, as he had previously decided, Caesar ordered two lines to drive off the enemy, the third to complete the work. When the camp was fortified, he left two legions there and a part of the auxiliaries; the remaining four legions he led back to the larger camp.

CHAPTER 50

THE NEXT DAY, in accordance with his usual practice, Caesar led out his forces from both camps, and advancing a little from the larger camp, he drew up a line of battle, and gave the enemy an opportunity to fight. When he perceived that they did not even then come forth, about noon he led his army back into camp. Then at last Ariovistus sent a part of his troops to attack the smaller camp. Fiercely the battle raged on both sides till the evening. At sunset, after many wounds had been inflicted and received, Ariovistus led his forces back into camp. When Caesar inquired of the prisoners why Ariovistus would not fight a decisive battle, he discovered this reason. Among the Germans it was customary for their matrons to declare by lots and prophetic utterances whether it was expedient to engage in battle or not; they declared that it was not fated that the Germans should conquer, if they engaged in battle before the new moon.

CHAPTER 51

THE NEXT DAY Caesar left what he considered a sufficient force as a garrison for each camp and drew up all the auxiliaries in full view of the enemy in front of the smaller camp, in order to use the auxiliaries for show because his legionary soldiers were numerically weak by comparison with the number of the enemy. Then, in a triple line of battle, he advanced up to the camp of the enemy. Now at last, of necessity, the Germans led their forces out of camp and drew up at equal intervals by tribes, the Harudes, Marcomani, Triboci, Vangiones, Nemetes, Sedusii, and Suebi. They hemmed in their whole line with carts and wagons, so that there might be no hope in flight. Upon these wagons they placed their women who, with tears and outstretched hands, entreated the men as they set out to battle not to deliver them into slavery to the Romans.

CHAPTER 52

CAESAR PLACED IN COMMAND of each of five legions a lieutenant, and a quaestor in command of the sixth in order that every man might have them as witnesses to his valor; he himself began the battle on the right wing, because he had noticed that that part of the enemy was the weakest. When the signal was given, our men attacked so vigorously and the enemy rushed forward so suddenly and swiftly that there was no time to hurl javelins at them. Our men therefore threw aside their javelins and fought at close quarters with their swords. But the Germans, according to their custom, quickly formed a phalanx and withstood the attack of our swords. Many of our men were found who leaped upon the phalanx, pulled back the shields from the hands of the enemy, and wounded them from above. Although the army of the enemy was routed on their left wing and put to flight, on their right wing they pressed our line hard by their great numbers. When young Publius Crassus who commanded the cavalry noticed this, as he was freer to act than those who were busy fighting, he sent the third line to the relief of our men who were hard pressed.

CHAPTER 53

THUS THE BATTLE WAS RENEWED, and all the enemy fled, and did not stop fleeing until they reached the Rhine, about fifteen miles from that place. There a very few, either, relying on their strength, tried to swim across, or, coming upon boats, found safety for themselves. Among these was Ariovistus, who, finding a small boat tied to the bank, escaped in it; our cavalry pursued all the rest and killed them. There were two wives of Ariovistus, one a Swabian by birth, whom he had brought with him from home, the other a Norican, sister of King Voccio, whom he had married in Gaul, after she had been sent to him by her brother; both perished in that flight. There were two daughters; of these one was killed, the other captured. When Gaius Valerius Procillus, bound with three chains, was being dragged along by his guards in the flight, he met Caesar himself, as he was pursuing the enemy with his cavalry. And indeed this circumstance brought Caesar no less pleasure than the victory itself, because he saw a most honorable man of the Province of Gaul, his close friend and guest, snatched from the hands of the enemy and restored to him, and because he felt that fortune had not detracted anything from his great pleasure and reason for thankfulness by the death of his friend. Procillus said that in his own presence the lots had been consulted three times to decide whether he should be burned at once or saved for another time; thanks to the lots he was unharmed. Marcus Metius was also found and brought back to Caesar.

CHAPTER 54

WHEN THE NEWS of this battle was carried across the Rhine, the Suebi, who had come to the banks of the river, began to return home; when those who dwell next to the Rhine perceived that they were panic-stricken, they pursued and killed a great number of them. Having finished two very great wars in one summer, Caesar led his army into winter quarters among the Sequani a little earlier than the season of the year required; he placed Labienus in charge of the winter quarters, and he himself set out for Cisalpine Gaul to hold court.

BOOK II

CHAPTER 1

WHEN CAESAR WAS in Cisalpine Gaul, as we have shown above, frequent reports were brought to him, and he was also informed by dispatches from Labienus that all the Belgae, who we had said constituted a third part of Gaul, were conspiring against the Roman people and were exchanging hostages. The reasons given for the conspiracy were these: In the first place, they were afraid that if all Gaul was subdued, our army would be led against them; in the second place, they were being stirred up by some Gauls, partly by those who had been unwilling that the Germans should remain any longer in Gaul and were now seriously objecting that the army of the Roman people should pass the winter and should become established in Gaul, partly by those who by reason of temperamental instability and fickleness were eager for a change of rulers. They were also being stirred up by others, because the supreme power in Gaul was generally seized by the more powerful chiefs and by those who had the means to hire men, and these could less easily effect that object under our sovereignty.

CHAPTER 2

DISTURBED BY THESE REPORTS and dispatches, Caesar enrolled two new legions in Cisalpine Gaul, and at the beginning of the summer he sent his lieutenant, Quintus Pedius, to lead them into Transalpine Gaul. As soon as a supply of fodder began to appear, he joined the army in person. He directed the Senones and the rest of the Gauls who were neighbors of the Belgae to find out what was going on among the Belgae and to keep him informed about these matters. All these unanimously reported that bodies of troops were being collected and that an army was being led into one place. Then, indeed, he thought that he ought not to hesitate to move against them. Having provided a supply of grain, he broke camp, and in about fifteen days he reached the territory of the Belgae.

CHAPTER 3

WHEN HE HAD COME there unexpectedly and more quickly than anyone had anticipated, the Remi, the tribe of the Belgae nearest to Gaul, sent to him as envoys Iccius and Andecumborius, the leading men of the state, to tell him that they surrendered themselves and all their possessions to the protection and power of the Roman people, that they had neither plotted with the rest of the Belgae, nor conspired against the Roman people, and that they were ready to give hostages, to obey his orders, to admit him into their towns, and to assist him with grain and other

supplies. All the rest of the Belgae, they said, were
under arms, and the Germans, who lived on this side
of the Rhine, had joined with them, and so great was
the fury of all of them that the Remi could not restrain
even the Suessiones, their own brothers and blood-rela-
tives, who enjoyed the same rights and laws and who
had the same government and the same magistrates as
themselves, from uniting with them.

CHAPTER 4

WHEN CAESAR INQUIRED of them what
states were under arms, what was their size and their
military strength, he learned the following facts: Most
of the Belgae had sprung from the Germans, and a
long while ago had been led across the Rhine and had
settled there on account of the productiveness of the
soil, and had driven out the Gauls who inhabited those
regions. They were the only people who, in the memory of our fathers, when all Gaul was ravaged, had prevented the Teutoni and the Cimbri from entering
their territory; and in consequence of the recollection
of this achievement they assumed great authority and
great airs in military matters. The Remi said that they
possessed complete information about their numbers
because, being united with them by blood relationships
and intermarriages, they had learned how large a contingent each representative had promised for that war
in the general council of the Belgae. Among them,
they said, the Bellovaci were the most powerful in
valor, influence, and the number of men; these could
muster a hundred thousand armed men, and out of

this number had promised sixty thousand picked men, and demanded for themselves the command of the whole war. The Suessiones were their neighbors; they possessed very extensive lands and very productive fields. Among them, even in our memory, their king had been Diviciacus, the most powerful man of all Gaul, who controlled not only a large part of these regions, but also of Britain. Now Galba was king; upon him, on account of his justice and good judgment, was conferred the supreme command by general consent; the Suessiones had twelve towns, and promised fifty thousand armed men; the Nervii, who were considered the fiercest among them and lived farthest away, had promised just as many; the Atrebates fifteen thousand, the Ambiani ten thousand, the Morini twenty-five thousand, the Menapii seven thousand, the Caleti ten thousand, the Veliocasses and the Viromandui just as many, the Atuatuci nineteen thousand; the Condrusi, the Eburones, the Caerosi, the Paemani, who are called by the common name of Germani, could, as they thought, arm about forty thousand men.

CHAPTER 5

CAESAR ADDRESSED the Remi in encouraging and gracious terms and ordered their entire senate to assemble before him and the children of their leading men to be brought to him as hostages. All these instructions were carried out by them carefully and promptly. He himself, in an earnest appeal to Diviciacus, the Aeduan, showed him how important it was for the Roman state and for their mutual welfare that the

forces of the enemy be kept apart, that it might not be
necessary to fight with so large a number at one time.
This could be done if the Aedui led their forces into
the territory of the Bellovaci and began to lay waste
their land. With these instructions he dismissed him.
When he heard that all the forces of the Belgae had
been gathered into one place and were advancing
against him, and when he learned from the scouts that
he had sent forward and from the Remi that the enemy
was not far away, he hastened to lead his army across
the Axona, which is in the most remote part of the
country of the Remi, and pitched camp there. Now this
movement helped him fortify one side of the camp by
the banks of the river, and rendered his rear safe from
the enemy; it also made it possible for supplies to be
brought from the Remi and the rest of the states.
Across that river there was a bridge. There he placed
a guard, and on the other side of the river he left the
lieutenant Quintus Titurius Sabinus with six cohorts;
he ordered him to construct a camp with a rampart
twelve feet high and a trench eighteen feet wide.

CHAPTER 6

EIGHT MILES from this camp was a
town of the Remi called Bibrax. From their line of
march the Belgae began to attack this town with great
violence. The defense was maintained with difficulty
on that day. The method of attack by the Gauls, the
same as that of the Belgae, is as follows: When a large
number of men is placed all around the fortifications,
and from all sides stones begin to be thrown at the

wall, and the wall is stripped of its defenders, they make a tortoise roof, advance to the gates, and undermine the wall. This was easily done on the present occasion. For since so large a number were hurling stones and darts, no one was able to stand upon the wall. When night had put an end to the assault, Iccius, one of the Remi, a man of the highest rank and influence among his countrymen, who was the officer in charge of the town, one of those who had come to Caesar as envoys to sue for peace, sent a message to Caesar to the effect that unless assistance were sent to their relief, they could not hold out any longer.

CHAPTER 7

ABOUT MIDNIGHT, using as guides the same men who had come as envoys from Iccius, Caesar sent to Bibrax Numidian and Cretan bowmen and Balearic slingers to relieve the inhabitants of the town; on their arrival, the Remi were inspired with the hope of repelling the assault and with an eager desire to take the offensive, and for the same reason the enemy gave up the hope of capturing the town. They halted for a short time near the town, laid waste the country of the Remi and set fire to all the villages and buildings which they could approach, and then hastened with all their forces to the camp of Caesar, and pitched their camp less than two miles away. This camp, as was indicated by the smoke and fires, extended more than eight miles in breadth.

CHAPTER 8

AT FIRST, because of the great number of the enemy and their extraordinary reputation for bravery, Caesar determined to refrain from battle. Daily, however, by cavalry skirmishes he kept trying to find out the prowess of the enemy and the courage of his own men. He discovered that our men were not inferior. The space in front of the camp was naturally convenient and suitable for forming a line of battle, because the hill on which the camp had been pitched rose gradually from the plain and extended in front over as much ground as a line of battle would require. On either side it offered steep slopes, while in front with a gentle slope it descended gradually to the level of the plain. On either side of the hill, Caesar extended a trench of about four hundred paces crosswise, and at the ends of the trench he constructed forts, and placed his artillery there, so that, after he had drawn up his line, the enemy, since they were so strong in numbers, while fighting on the flanks, might not be able to surround his men. When this was done, he left in camp the two legions he had recently enrolled, so that, if need should arise at any point, they might be brought up as a reserve force, and he drew up the remaining six legions in line of battle before the camp. The enemy likewise had led their forces out of camp and had drawn them up.

CHAPTER 9

BETWEEN OUR ARMY and that of the enemy there was a marsh of no great size. The enemy were waiting to see whether our men would cross it; but our men were ready in arms to attack them while they were in difficulties if they should be the first to attempt to cross. Meanwhile a cavalry engagement continued between the two lines. When neither side began to cross the marsh and the cavalry engagement favored our side, Caesar led his troops back to camp. The enemy at once hastened from that place to the river Axona, which, as has been shown, was behind our camp. There they discovered fords and tried to lead a part of their forces across, intending to storm, if they could, the fort commanded by the lieutenant Quintus Titurius, and to break down the bridge; but if they could not do that, to lay waste the lands of the Remi, which were of great service to us in the conduct of the war, and to cut off our men from supplies.

CHAPTER 10

ON BEING INFORMED of this by Titurius, Caesar led all his cavalry and light-armed Numidians, the slingers and the archers, across the bridge, and hastened against the enemy. There was fierce fighting in that place. Our men, attacking the encumbered enemy in the river, slew a great number of them. As the rest were trying most courageously to cross over the bodies of the slain, the Romans drove them back

with a shower of missiles; those of the soldiers who
had crossed the river were surrounded and slain by our
cavalry. The enemy realized that they had been disappointed in their hope of storming the town and of crossing the river, and saw that our men were not advancing to a less favorable position for the sake of fighting.
As their own grain supply began to fail, they summoned a council of war and decided that it was best
for each man to return home, and then to assemble
from all quarters to defend those into whose territory
the Romans should first lead their army, so that they
might fight in their own territory rather than in that
of others, and that they might use their own supplies
of grain. Besides the other reasons, also this consideration led them to this decision; they knew that Diviciacus and the Aedui were approaching the territory of
the Bellovaci, who could not be persuaded to stay any
longer and not bring aid to their own people.

CHAPTER 11

HAVING REACHED this decision, they
marched out of camp at the second watch, with great
uproar and confusion, without a fixed order and without discipline, since each one sought for himself the
first place on the road and was in a hurry to reach
home, so that they made their departure look like a
rout. Caesar learned of this immediately through
scouts; but since he feared an ambush because he had
not yet discovered for what reason they were departing,
he kept his army and cavalry in camp. At daybreak,
when the fact was confirmed by scouts, he sent forward all the cavalry to delay the rear guard of the en-

emy. He placed the lieutenants Quintus Pedius and Lucius Aurunculeius Cotta in command of this cavalry; and he ordered the lieutenant Titus Labienus to follow closely with three legions. These men, attacking the rear guard and pursuing them for many miles, killed a great number of them as they fled. While those at the rear, to whom the Roman soldiers had come, made a stand and bravely sustained the attack of our soldiers, those in front, because they appeared to be free from danger and were not restrained by any compulsion or command, when they heard the shouting, broke ranks, and all sought safety for themselves in flight. Thus, without any risk, our men killed as great a number of them as daylight permitted. At sunset they stopped and, in accordance with their orders, returned to camp.

CHAPTER 12

THE NEXT DAY, before the enemy could recover from their terror and flight, Caesar led his army into the territory of the Suessiones, next to the Remi, and by a forced march hastened to the town of Noviodunum. He tried to assault it immediately after his arrival, because he heard that it was destitute of defenders, but though the defenders were few, he was not able to take it by storm on account of the width of the ditch and the height of the wall. Therefore, having fortified his camp, he began to move forward the arbor sheds and to get ready the equipment that was necessary for assault. Meanwhile, the whole body of the Suessiones, after their flight, came into the town on the following night. When the arbor sheds were speedily moved up to the town, a mound thrown up, and towers built, the Gauls, alarmed by the size of the siege-works, which they had not seen or heard of before, and by the speed of the Romans, sent envoys to Caesar to ask for terms of surrender. The Remi asked that the Suessiones should be spared, and their request was granted.

CHAPTER 13

CAESAR ACCEPTED as hostages the foremost men of the state and also the two sons of King Galba himself, and, after all the arms had been delivered up from the town, he accepted the surrender of the Suessiones and led his army into the territory of the Bellovaci. When these had gathered with all their possessions in the town of Bratuspantium, and Caesar with his army was about five miles from that place, all the old men came out of the town, and began to stretch out their hands to Caesar and to signify by their voices that they were submitting themselves to his protection and power, and were no longer struggling in arms against the Roman people. Likewise, when he had come up to the town and was pitching camp there, the children and women stood on the wall and with outstretched hands, as was their custom, begged the Romans for peace.

CHAPTER 14

ON THEIR BEHALF, Diviciacus (after the retreat of the Belgae he had dismissed the forces of the Aedui and returned to Caesar) made the following plea: The Bellovaci had at all times enjoyed the protection and friendship of the Aeduan state. Incited by their chiefs, who kept saying that the Aedui, reduced to slavery by Caesar, were suffering every kind of ill-treatment and insult, they had both revolted from the Aedui and made war upon the Roman people. Those who had been the ringleaders of the plot, realizing how great a calamity they had brought upon the state, had fled to Britain. Not only the Bellovaci, but also the Aedui on their behalf, entreated him to show his well-known mercifulness and compassion towards them. If he did that, he would enhance the prestige of the Aedui among all the Belgae, with whose assistance and resources they had been accustomed to carry through any wars that had arisen.

CHAPTER 15

CAESAR SAID that out of regard for Divi-ciacus and the Aedui he would receive the Bellovaci under his protection and would spare them; but, as their state was of great influence among the Belgae and had the largest population, he demanded six hundred hostages. When these had been delivered, and all the arms had been collected from the town, Caesar left that place and came into the territory of the Ambiani; these surrendered themselves and their possessions without delay. The country of the Nervii adjoined the territory of the Ambiani; when Caesar inquired about their character and customs, he discovered the follow-ing: Traders had no access to them; they allowed no wine or other things which contribute to luxurious liv-ing to be imported, because they thought that these things weaken the spirit and impair the valor. They were fierce men and very courageous; they upbraided and condemned the rest of the Belgae, because they had surrendered to the Roman people and had cast away the courage of their forefathers. They affirmed that they would neither send envoys nor accept any terms of peace.

CHAPTER 16

WHEN CAESAR HAD ADVANCED three days through their territory, he found out from prisoners that the river Sabis was not more than ten miles from his camp, and that all the Nervii had encamped across that river, and together with their neighbors, the Atrebates and Viromandui, (for they had persuaded both these tribes to try the same fortune of war) were awaiting the arrival of the Romans; they were also awaiting the forces of the Atuatuci, which were on the way. Caesar also learned that they had put their women and those who, by reason of age, appeared useless for war in a place to which no army had any access because of the marshes.

CHAPTER 17

HAVING LEARNED THIS, Caesar sent forward scouts and centurions to choose a suitable place for a camp. When many of the Belgae who had surrendered and other Gauls attached themselves to Caesar and were marching with him, some of these, as was afterwards learned from prisoners, having observed the usual marching order of our army during those days, came by night to the Nervii and informed them that between the several legions there was a great quantity of baggage, and that, when the first legion had reached camp and the rest were a great distance away, it would be very easy to attack it while it was still carrying its packs; when this legion had been driven back, and the baggage had been plundered, the rest would not dare to make a stand. The plan of those who furnished the information was favored by the following circumstance. The Nervii, not being strong in cavalry (for even to this day they pay little attention to this branch of the service; all their strength lies in their infantry), long ago devised the following plan of hampering the cavalry of their neighbors, if they came to them in order to plunder. They cut into young trees and bent them over, letting the branches grow thickly sideways; in the intervening spaces they planted briers and thorns. Thus they made hedges which furnished a fortification like a wall, which could not be penetrated and not even seen through. Since the march of our army would be obstructed by these obstacles, the Nervii thought that the proposed plan should be tried.

CHAPTER 18

THE NATURAL FEATURES of the ground which our men had chosen for the camp were as follows: A hill, sloping evenly from the top, descended to the river Sabis, which we have mentioned above. From this river there rose another hill with a similar upward

slope, facing this hill and opposite to it, open for about
two hundred paces at its base, but wooded along the
upper portion, so that one could not easily see the interior. Within these woods the enemy kept themselves
in hiding; on the open ground along the river a few
pickets of cavalry were seen. The depth of the river
was about three feet.

CHAPTER 19

HAVING SENT his cavalry ahead, Caesar
followed with all his forces; but the arrangement and
order of the march were different from what the Belgae had reported to the Nervii. For when he was approaching an enemy, Caesar, in accordance with his
usual practice, led six legions in light order; behind
them he placed the baggage of the entire army; the
two newly enrolled legions brought up the rear and
served as a guard to the baggage train. Our cavalry
crossed the river with the slingers and archers, and
joined battle with the cavalry of the enemy. These retired repeatedly into the woods to their comrades, and,
coming out of the woods, again made an attack on our
soldiers. Our men did not dare pursue them, as they
retreated, farther than the limit of open ground. Meanwhile, the six legions which had been the first to arrive measured off the trench-work and began to fortify
the camp. When the first part of the baggage train of
our army was seen by those who lay hidden in the
woods (the time agreed upon among them for beginning the battle), the Nervii drew up their line and
formed their ranks within the woods; then, encourag-

ing one another, they rushed forward suddenly with all their forces and made an attack upon our cavalry. These were easily routed and thrown into confusion; then with incredible speed the enemy rushed down to the river, so that almost at the same instant they were seen near the woods, in the river, and close upon us. Then with the same speed they hastened up the hill towards our camp and attacked those who were engaged in the works.

CHAPTER 20

CAESAR HAD TO DO everything at one time: to raise the flag which was the signal for a general call to arms; to give the signal with the trumpet; to recall the soldiers from the trench-work; to summon those who had gone a little farther to seek material for the rampart; to draw up a line of battle; to encourage the soldiers; and to give the signal for battle. A great part of these duties could not be done because of the shortness of time and the onrush of the enemy. Two things served to offset these difficulties: the knowledge and experience of the soldiers (trained in previous battles, they could determine for themselves what ought to be done just as readily as others could have shown them) and the fact that Caesar had forbidden the several lieutenants to leave the work and their respective legions before the camp was fortified. These lieutenants, on account of the nearness and the speed of the enemy, did not then wait for orders from Caesar, but, on their own responsibility, took what steps seemed to them proper.

CHAPTER 21

HAVING GIVEN the indispensable orders, where chance led him Caesar ran down to encourage the soldiers, and came to the Tenth Legion. He addressed the soldiers but briefly; he urged them to bear in mind their former valor, not to be alarmed, and to withstand the attack of the enemy bravely. Then, as the enemy were no more than a spear's throw away, he gave the signal for battle. After he had gone to another quarter for the purpose of encouraging his men there, he found them already fighting. So short was the time, and so ready for battle was the spirit of the enemy that our men had no time to put on their decorations, or even to put on their helmets and to draw the covers off their shields. Whatever part of the line each soldier chanced to reach as he came from the trench-work, and whatever standards he caught sight of first, there he took his stand, so as not to lose time for fighting while seeking his own company.

CHAPTER 22

THE ARMY WAS DRAWN UP as the character of the ground, the slope of the hill, and the emergency of the moment required, rather than in accordance with the arrangement approved by military science. The legions were separated and were opposing the enemy, one at one point, another at another, and their view was obstructed by a barrier of very thick hedges, as we have shown above. For this reason reserves could not be posted at fixed points, and it could not be foreseen what would be needed in each section, and all the commands could not be given by one person. Therefore, under such disadvantageous conditions, diverse issues of fortune followed.

CHAPTER 23

THE SOLDIERS of the Ninth and the Tenth Legions, who were stationed on the left wing of the army, hurled their pikes, and from the higher ground speedily drove down to the river the Atrebates (the division which faced them), who were out of breath from running and fatigue and disabled by wounds, and pursuing them as they were attempting to cross, they killed with their swords a great part of them while they were in difficulties. They themselves did not hesitate to cross the river, and, having advanced to an unfavorable ground, when the enemy again offered resistance, renewed the battle and put them to flight. Likewise, in another quarter, two legions separately, the Eleventh and the Eighth, drove the Viromandui, whom they had engaged, from the higher ground and continued the battle upon the very banks of the river. Now almost the whole camp on the front and on the left side was unprotected, since the Twelfth Legion was stationed on the right wing and the Seventh at no great distance from it. All the Nervii, in a very dense column, led by Boduognatus, who held the supreme command, hastened to that spot; some of them began to surround the legions on their exposed flank, and others to make for the height on which the camp stood.

CHAPTER 24

AT THE SAME TIME our cavalry and light-armed infantry, who had been along with them, had been routed, as I had said, by the first assault of the enemy. When they were returning to camp, they met the enemy face to face and again sought flight in another direction. The camp followers, who from the rear gate and from the highest ridge of the hill had seen our victorious forces cross the river, had gone out to plunder. But when they looked back and saw the enemy moving about in our camp, they fled headlong. At the same time there arose the shouting and hubbub of those who were coming up with the baggage train, and panic-stricken, some rushed in one direction, others in another. All these events alarmed the cavalry of the Treveri, whose reputation for courage is extraordinary among the Gauls; they had been sent by their state to Caesar as auxiliaries. When they saw our camp filled with a large number of the enemy, the legions hard pressed and almost surrounded, the camp followers, horsemen, slingers, and Numidians separated and scattered and fleeing in all directions, they despaired of our fortunes and hastened home. They reported to their state that the Romans had been routed and conquered, and that the enemy had taken possession of their camp and baggage train.

CHAPTER 25

AFTER ENCOURAGING the Tenth Legion, Caesar proceeded to the right wing, where he saw that his men were hard pressed. The soldiers of the Twelfth Legion, since their standards had been collected in one place, were packed together so closely that they were hindering one another in fighting. All the centurions of the fourth cohort and the standard-bearer had been killed, and the standard was lost; almost all the centurions of the other cohorts were either wounded or killed; among them was the chief centurion, Publius Sextius Baculus, a very brave man, who was so exhausted by many severe wounds that he could no longer stand up. The rest were less active; some in the rear ranks had abandoned their position and were withdrawing from the battle and were trying to avoid the missiles. The enemy did not cease coming up in front from the lower ground, and were pressing hard on both flanks. Caesar saw that matters had reached a crisis and that there was no reserve force that could be sent up; therefore, snatching a shield from a soldier in the rear, because he himself had come there without a shield, he advanced to the first line, and calling on the centurions by name and encouraging the rest of the soldiers, he ordered them to advance and to open up the ranks, so that they could use their swords more easily. On his arrival, hope was brought to the soldiers, and their spirit was renewed; every one of them, even under conditions of the utmost peril to himself, desired to do his best under the eyes of the general. So the attack of the enemy was checked a little.

CHAPTER 26

WHEN CAESAR PERCEIVED that the Seventh Legion, which had taken its position nearby, was also hard pressed by the enemy, he instructed the tribunes of the soldiers to see to it that the two legions gradually draw together, face about, and advance against the enemy. When this was done, as the soldiers brought assistance to one another and did not fear that they would be surrounded in the rear by the enemy, they began to resist more boldly and to fight more bravely. Meanwhile the soldiers of the two legions which had acted as guard to the baggage-train in the rear, when the battle was reported to them, quickened their pace and were seen by the enemy on the top of the hill. When Titus Labienus, having taken possession of the camp of the enemy, saw from the higher ground what was going on in our camp, he sent the Tenth Legion to support our men. And when they had learned from the flight of the cavalry and the camp-followers how matters stood, and in how great danger the camp, the legions, and the commander were, they made the utmost possible speed.

CHAPTER 27

UPON THEIR ARRIVAL, so great a change in the situation was brought about that our men, even those who had fallen down exhausted by wounds, supported themselves on their shields and renewed the fight. Then the camp-followers, seeing the enemy panic-stricken, unarmed as they were, rushed against the armed enemy; moreover, the cavalry, that they might by valor wipe out the disgrace of their flight, tried to outdo the legionary soldiers at every point in fighting. But the enemy, even in utter despair of safety, displayed such great courage that when their front ranks had fallen, the next stood upon the fallen bodies and fought from them; when these too fell and their bodies were piled up in heaps, those who survived continued to hurl javelins against our men as from a mound, and caught and threw back our javelins. Therefore, we should not conclude that men of such great courage in vain dared to cross a very broad river, to climb very steep banks, and to go up to a very unfavorable place—tasks which, in themselves most difficult, their heroic courage had made easy.

CHAPTER 28

AT THE END of this battle the nation and name of the Nervii had been almost reduced to utter destruction. When the report of this battle reached their old men, who, as we had mentioned, had been gathered with the women and children in the tidal marshes and swamps, since they supposed that there was nothing to stop the victors and nothing to protect the vanquished, with the consent of all the survivors, they sent envoys to Caesar and surrendered to him. In relating the disaster of their state, they said that from six hundred senators they had been reduced to three, and from sixty thousand men to barely five hundred who could bear arms. In order that he might be seen to use compassion towards the wretched and the suppliant, Caesar spared them most carefully; he ordered them to keep their own territory and towns, and commanded their neighbors to restrain themselves and their dependents from doing any wrong or injury to the Nervii.

CHAPTER 29

WHEN THE ATUATUCI, of whom we have written above, were coming with all their forces to the assistance of the Nervii and heard of this battle, they left their march and returned home. Abandoning all their towns and forts, they gathered all their possessions in one stronghold, which was admirably fortified by nature. Although this place on all sides round about had very high cliffs and slopes, on one side there was a gently rising approach, not more than two hundred feet wide. This place they had fortified with a very high double wall; upon it they were placing stones of great weight and beams sharpened at the ends. The Atuatuci were descended from the Cimbri and the Teutoni. Upon their march into our Province and Italy, these two tribes deposited on this side of the Rhine such of their cattle and goods as they could not drive or carry with them, and left six thousand of their men as a guard and a garrison. After the destruction of their countrymen, these men, having been harassed for many years by their neighbors, sometimes waging an offensive war, at other times a defensive war, by general agreement made peace, and chose this district as their permanent home.

CHAPTER 30

ON THE ARRIVAL of our army, the Atua-
tuci made frequent sallies from the stronghold, and
engaged in skirmishes with our men; afterwards,
closed in by a rampart twelve feet high and fifteen
thousand feet in circumference, and numerous forts,
they kept themselves within the town. When the *vineae*
had been brought up and an embankment had been
built, and when they saw a tower set up at a distance,
the Atuatuci at first, standing on the wall, laughed at
us and made taunting remarks because so big an engine was being erected so far off. With what sort of
hands, said they, by what strength could men of such
small size (for, as a rule, our small stature, by comparison with the great size of their bodies, is held in contempt by the Gauls) hope to be able to place a tower of
such great weight on the wall?

CHAPTER 31

BUT WHEN THEY SAW that the tower
was moving and approaching the walls, alarmed at the
strange and unwonted sight, they sent envoys to Caesar
to ask for peace. These spoke as follows: They did not
suppose that the Romans waged war without the help
of the gods, since they were able to move forward at
such great speed engines of so great a height; they
therefore submitted themselves and all they had to the
Roman power. One thing only they begged him not to
do: If, in accordance with his mercy and kindness,

which they kept hearing about from others, Caesar should perhaps decide to spare the Atuatuci, he should not deprive them of their arms. Nearly all their neighbors were their enemies, and were jealous of their courage; they would be unable to defend themselves against them if they delivered up their arms. It would be better for them, if they should be reduced to such a condition, to suffer any lot whatever at the hands of the Roman people than to be tortured and slain by those among whom they had been accustomed to exercise dominion.

CHAPTER 32

TO THIS APPEAL Caesar replied that, in accordance with his practice rather than for any deserts on their part, he would spare their state if they surrendered before the battering-ram touched their wall; but there could be no terms of surrender unless their arms were delivered up. He would do what he had done in the case of the Nervii, and command their neighbors not to do any harm to those who had surrendered to the Roman people. When this was reported to their people, they said that they would obey his commands. A great quantity of arms was thrown down from the wall into the trench which was before the town, so many that the heaps of weapons almost reached the full height of the wall and of the rampart, but they concealed and kept back in the town, as was afterwards discovered, about a third part. They threw open the gates and enjoyed peace on that day.

CHAPTER 33

TOWARDS EVENING Caesar ordered the gates to be closed and the soldiers to go out of the town, in order that the townspeople might not suffer any harm from his soldiers during the night. But the townspeople had previously formed a plot, as was afterwards learned. Since they believed that after the surrender our men would withdraw the outposts, or at any rate maintain them with less care, some, with those arms which they had retained and concealed, others with shields made of bark or wickerwork, which they had hastily covered over with skins (as the shortness of time required), in the third watch with all their forces suddenly made a sally from the town, where the ascent to our fortifications seemed least steep. The warning was speedily given by fire-signals, as Caesar had previously ordered, and the soldiers from the nearest forts rushed to that point. The enemy fought fiercely, as brave men were bound to fight in utter despair of safety, on unfavorable ground, against those who were throwing missiles from a rampart and from towers, since all hope of safety lay in courage alone. About four thousand men were slain, and the rest were forced back into the town. Next day the gates were burst in, as there was no longer anyone to defend them, and our soldiers were sent in; then Caesar sold the booty of the town in one lot. The purchasers reported that the number of persons was fifty-three thousand.

CHAPTER 34

AT THE SAME TIME Caesar was informed by Publius Crassus, whom he had sent with one legion against the Veneti, the Venelli, the Osismi, the Coriosolites, the Esuvii, the Aulerci, and the Redones, maritime states which border on the Atlantic Ocean, that all these states had been brought under the authority and power of the Roman people.

CHAPTER 35

WHEN ALL GAUL had been subdued by these achievements, so impressive a report of this war was carried to the natives that envoys were sent to Caesar by those tribes who lived across the Rhine, to promise that they would give hostages and obey his commands. As Caesar was hastening to Italy and Illyricum, he ordered these envoys to return to him at the beginning of the next summer. After the legions had been led into winter quarters among the Carnutes, the Andes, and the Turoni, and such states as were near those regions in which he had waged war, he himself set out for Italy. Upon receipt of Caesar's dispatches, a solemn thanksgiving of fifteen days was decreed to celebrate his achievements, an honor which before that time had been conferred upon no one.

BOOK III

CHAPTER 1

WHEN CAESAR WAS SETTING OUT for
Italy, he sent Servius Galba with the Twelfth Legion
and a part of the cavalry to the countries of the Nantuates, the Veragri, and the Seduni, which extend from
the territory of the Allobroges and Lake Geneva and
from the river Rhone to the highest part of the Alps.
The reason for sending him was his intention to open
up the route through the Alps, through which traders
had been accustomed to travel at great risk and on payment of heavy tolls. He permitted Galba to station his
legion in these places for the winter, if he thought it
necessary. Galba fought several successful battles with
the enemy and took by storm a number of their forts;
after envoys were sent to him from all sides and hostages had been given, a peace was concluded. Galba
then determined to station two cohorts in the country
of the Nantuates, and to winter himself with the remaining cohorts of that legion in a village of the Veragri called Octodurus. This village, set in a valley, with
a small plain adjoining, is bounded on all sides by very
lofty mountains. As it was divided in two by a river,
Galba assigned one half of it to the Gauls, and reserved
the other, which they had evacuated, for the cohorts to
winter in. He fortified this place with a rampart and a
ditch.

CHAPTER 2

WHEN SEVERAL DAYS had passed in winter quarters, and Galba had ordered grain to be brought in, he was suddenly informed by scouts that during the night all the Gauls had left that part of the village which he had allotted to them and that the mountains which overhung were occupied by a very large force of the Seduni and the Veragri. Several reasons had led the Gauls suddenly to adopt the plan of renewing the war and crushing the legion. In the first place, because of its small numbers they looked with contempt upon the legion, which, in addition, lacked its full strength, as two cohorts had been withdrawn and many individuals were absent who had been sent to seek provisions. In the second place, they thought that because of the disadvantageous position of the Romans, when they themselves should rush down from the mountains into the valley and hurl their missiles, not even their first attack could be withstood. Besides, they were indignant that their children had been taken away from them under the name of hostages; and they were convinced that the Romans were trying to seize the summits of the Alps and to annex those parts to the neighboring Province, not only for the sake of the passes, but also for the sake of securing a permanent possession.

CHAPTER 3

UPON RECEIVING this information, Galba speedily summoned a council of war and asked for opinions. The work on the winter quarters and the fortifications were not quite completed, and sufficient provision had not been made for grain and other supplies, because after the surrender of the enemy and the receipt of hostages Galba thought that he had no occasion to fear hostilities. The serious danger that faced them had arisen suddenly and unexpectedly; by this time almost all the higher places were seen packed with a multitude of armed men, and no help could come and no supplies could be brought up because the roads were blocked. When hope of safety was almost despaired of, several members of the council voiced the opinion that they leave their baggage, make a sally, and try to gain safety by the same routes by which they had come there. But the majority decided to reserve this plan to the last, and meanwhile to await the outcome and to defend the camp.

CHAPTER 4

AFTER A BRIEF INTERVAL, so brief that it hardly allowed time for making those arrangements and carrying out those measures which had been determined upon, the enemy at a given signal rushed down from all sides and hurled stones and javelins upon the rampart. At first, our men, with their strength unimpaired, resisted them bravely and did not cast a missile in vain from their higher station; and when any part of the camp, stripped of defenders, seemed to be hard pressed, to that part they rushed and brought aid. But on this account they were at a disadvantage; when the enemy, exhausted by prolonged fighting, retired from the battle, others with fresh strength were taking their places. But nothing of this sort could be done by our men, on account of their small numbers; not only was it impossible for an exhausted soldier to retire from the battle, but not even a wounded soldier could leave the spot where he had taken his stand to look after himself.

CHAPTER 5

WHEN FIGHTING had been going on continually for more than six hours, our men lacked not only strength, but also weapons; the enemy, on the other hand, were pressing on more fiercely, and, as our men became weaker, began to destroy the rampart and to fill in the trenches. At this critical moment, Publius Sextius Baculus, a centurion of the first rank, who, we have mentioned, had been disabled by many wounds in the battle with the Nervii, and likewise Gaius Volusenus, a tribune of the soldiers, a man of excellent judgment and courage, hastened to Galba and pointed out to him that the only hope of safety was to try the last resource by making a sally through the enemy's lines. Therefore, Galba summoned the centurions and immediately directed the soldiers to stop fighting for a short time, and only to intercept the missiles hurled by the enemy, and to try to recover their strength from their exertions; then, upon a given signal, to burst forth from the camp, and place all hope of safety in courage.

CHAPTER 6

THE SOLDIERS CARRIED OUT these orders, and, suddenly making a sally from all the gates, gave the enemy no chance either to find out what was taking place or to rally. So there was a change of fortune. Our men surrounded on all sides and cut off those who had entertained the hope of capturing the camp. Of over thirty thousand men (that was the number of the natives reported to have come against the camp) more than a third were killed; the rest, panic-stricken, were put to flight, and were not allowed to rally even on the higher ground. Thus, all the forces of the enemy were routed and stripped of their arms, and the Roman soldiers retired to their camp and fortifications. After this battle, Galba was unwilling to tempt fortune too often; since he remembered that he had come into winter quarters with one design, but saw that he had found conditions different, he was greatly concerned by the lack of grain and supplies. Therefore, on the next day he set fire to all the buildings of that village, and started to hasten back to the Province; as no enemy hindered or delayed his march, he brought the legion back safely into the territory of the Nantuates, and from there into that of the Allobroges, where he passed the winter.

CHAPTER 7

AFTER THESE EVENTS, Caesar had every reason to think that Gaul was at peace, for the Belgae had been defeated, the Germans expelled, and the Seduni conquered in the Alps. Therefore at the beginning of winter he set out for Illyricum, because he wished to visit also these tribes and to become acquainted with these regions. But suddenly war broke out again in Gaul. The cause of this war was the following: Young Publius Crassus together with the Seventh Legion was wintering near the Atlantic Ocean, in the country of the Andes. As there was a scarcity of grain in those parts, he sent subsidiary officers and military tribunes to several neighboring states to seek grain and supplies. Among these officers Titus Terrasidius was sent to the Esuvii, Marcus Trebius Gallus to the Coriosolites, and Quintus Velanius with Titus Silius to the Veneti.

CHAPTER 8

OF ALL THE COUNTRIES on the whole seacoast, the Veneti have by far the greatest influence, for they have many ships in which they are accustomed to sail to Britain, and they excel all the other tribes in the theory and practice of navigation. Since the violence of the open sea is great, and they themselves hold the harbors which are few and far between, the Veneti levy tolls on almost all those who are accustomed to sail that sea. They took the first step by detaining Silius and Velanius, for they thought that through them they would recover the hostages whom they had given to Crassus. Their neighbors, influenced by their example, (for the decisions of the Gauls are sudden and unexpected) detained Trebius and Terrasidius for the same reason; and after rapidly dispatching envoys, through their chiefs they bound themselves by mutual oath to do nothing except by common consent and to share the same issue of their fortune. Moreover, they urged the other states to preserve the liberty which they had inherited from their ancestors, rather than to prefer to endure Roman slavery. The whole seacoast was quickly won to their opinion, and they sent a joint embassy to Publius Crassus, bidding him to restore their hostages if he wished to recover his officers.

CHAPTER 9

WHEN CAESAR WAS INFORMED of these matters by Crassus, because he was too far away, he ordered warships to be built meanwhile on the river Loire, which flows into the Atlantic Ocean, rowers to be drafted from the Province, and sailors and steersmen to be assembled. These orders were quickly carried out, and as soon as the season of the year permitted, he himself hastened to the army. When the Veneti and also the other states were informed of Caesar's arrival, because they realized how great an offense they had committed by detaining and imprisoning envoys (a title which had always been held sacred and inviolable among all nations), they began to prepare for war on a scale proportionate to the magnitude of their danger, and especially to provide naval equipment. On this ac-

count they had greater hope of success because they
had much confidence in the natural features of their
country. They knew that the land routes were cut by
inlets of the sea, that our navigation could be hampered
by the lack of knowledge of the country and by the
scarcity of harbors, and they were confident that our
armies would be unable to remain long among them because of lack of grain. And even though everything
should turn out contrary to their expectation, yet they
had a very powerful navy, while the Romans had no
supply of ships, and were unacquainted with the
shoals, harbors, and islands in the regions where they
were about to wage war. And they saw that navigation
on a land-locked sea was far different from what it was
on a very vast and open Ocean. Adopting this plan,·
they fortified their towns, brought in grain from the
fields, and assembled as many ships as possible in Ve-
netia, where it was certain that Caesar would begin his
campaign. They took as allies for that war the Osismi,
the Lexovii, the Namnetes, the Ambiliati, the Morini,
the Diablintes, and the Menapii; they summoned auxiliaries from Britain, which lies opposite those regions.

CHAPTER 10

IN SPITE of the above-mentioned difficulties of carrying on a war, many considerations spurred
Caesar on to undertake it: the wrong done by the de-
tention of Roman knights, the renewal of war after
their surrender, the revolt after hostages had been
given, the conspiracy of so many states, but above all
the fear that if this part of Gaul were not dealt with,

the other nations might think that the same course of action was open to them. Therefore, since he realized that almost all the Gauls were eager for a change of rule, and were easily and quickly provoked to war, and that all men naturally love liberty and hate the state of slavery, he thought that he ought to divide his army and distribute it more widely before more states should league together.

CHAPTER 11

THEREFORE, HE SENT the lieutenant Titus Labienus with the cavalry into the territory of the Treveri, who live next to the river Rhine. He ordered him to proceed to the Remi and the rest of the Belgae, and to keep them in allegiance, and to stop the Germans, who were said to have been summoned by the Belgae to their aid, if they should attempt to force the passage of the river in boats. He ordered Publius Crassus to proceed to Aquitania with twelve legionary cohorts and a large body of cavalry, in order that auxiliaries might not be sent into Gaul from these tribes, and such powerful tribes might not be united. He sent the lieutenant Quintus Titurius with three legions to the territory of the Venelli, the Coriosolites, and the Lexovii, in order to keep their forces at a distance. Young Decimus Brutus was put in command of the fleet and the Gallic ships which he ordered to assemble from the territory of the Pictones, the Santoni, and the other pacified regions, and ordered him to proceed to the country of the Veneti as soon as he could. Caesar himself hastened there with the infantry.

CHAPTER 12

THE TOWNS OF THE VENETI were as a rule situated at the ends of tongues of land and promontories, so that they could not be approached by land when the tide had rushed in from the sea (which regularly happened every twelve hours); and they could not be approached by ships because in ebb-tide the ships would be damaged in shallow water. Thus, both of these conditions hindered the storming of their towns; whenever the inhabitants of the town were overcome by our huge siege-works (when the sea had been shut out by our massive dikes which were built up to a level with the walls of the town), they began to despair of their fortunes; then, bringing up a large number of ships, of which they had a very great supply, they would carry off in them all their possessions and retire to the nearest towns; there they would defend themselves again with the same advantages of position. During a great part of the summer they did this the more easily because our ships were held back by storms, and because the difficulty of sailing on a vast and open sea, with its strong tides and an almost total lack of harbors, was very great.

CHAPTER 13

THE VENETI did not experience the same difficulty in navigating these waters, for their ships were built and equipped in the following fashion: Their keels were considerably flatter than those of our ships, in order that they might more easily cope with the shoals and the ebb-tide; their prows were very high, adapted to the force of sea waves and storms; their ships were built entirely of oak, to endure great violence and buffeting; the crosstimbers, made of beams a foot thick, were fastened to the sides with iron bolts as thick as a man's thumb; the anchors were secured by iron chains instead of ropes. They used sails made of hides and leather dressed thin, either because of their lack of flax and their ignorance of its use, or, more probably, because they thought that such strong storms on the Atlantic Ocean and such violent gusts of wind could not be withstood by ordinary sails, and such heavy vessels could not conveniently be managed by means of sails. The encounter of our fleet with these ships was such that our fleet excelled only in speed and propulsion by oars; other conditions, in regard to the nature of the place and the force of the storms, were more suited and favorable to them. For our ships could not damage them by ramming (their solidity was so great), and, on account of their height, a missile could not easily be hurled, and for the same reason they were less readily held with grappling hooks. There was the further advantage that whenever the wind began to blow a gale and they ran before the wind, they would weather the storm more easily and ride in shallow water more safely, and when left by the tide they felt no fear of rocks and reefs; but our ships had to fear greatly the chance of all these occurrences.

CHAPTER 14

AFTER CAESAR HAD TAKEN several towns by storm, he realized that so much labor was being spent in vain and that the flight of the enemy could not be checked by the capture of their towns, and that no harm could be done them. He therefore decided that he must wait for his fleet. As soon as it arrived and was sighted by the enemy, about two hundred and twenty of their ships, fully prepared and completely fitted out with every kind of equipment, sailed out of the harbor, and took up stations opposite ours. And it was not quite clear to Brutus, who commanded the fleet, or to the tribunes of the soldiers and the centurions, to whom individual ships had been assigned, what to do or what plan of battle to adopt. For they knew that the enemy's ships could not be damaged by ramming; moreover, even though turrets had been erected on the Roman ships, the height of the sterns of the Gallic ships exceeded these, so that from the lower level of our ships missiles could not be hurled effectively, while those hurled by the Gauls fell with greater force. But one device made ready beforehand by our men was very useful—sharp-pointed hooks fixed into the ends of long poles and fastened to them, of a shape not unlike that of siege hooks. Whenever the ropes which fastened the sail yards to the masts were caught by them and pulled taut, when our ship was driven forward vigorously, the ropes were severed. And when these were cut, the sail yards of necessity fell down, so that, since in the case of the Gallic ships all hope lay in their sails and rigging, when these were taken away, all control of the ships was taken away at the same time. The rest of the contest depended on courage, in which our soldiers easily had the advantage, the more so because the struggle took place in sight of Caesar and of the entire army, so that no unusually brave deed could be unobserved. For all the hills and higher places from which there was a near view over the sea were occupied by the Roman army.

CHAPTER 15

WHEN THE SAIL YARDS had been torn down, as we have described, two or three of our ships would surround a single ship of the enemy, and the soldiers would make every effort to board it. When the natives saw what was happening, since after the capture of many of their ships no remedy could be discovered against these tactics, they hastened to seek safety in flight. And now their ships turned in that direction in which the wind was blowing, when suddenly so great a calm and stillness fell that they could not stir from the spot. Now this circumstance was exceedingly favorable to complete our victory; for our men, pursuing their ships, took them one by one, so that, when night came on, of all their number very few gained land after a battle that lasted from the fourth hour till sunset.

CHAPTER 16

BY THIS ENGAGEMENT the war with the Veneti and the whole sea-coast was successfully finished. For not only had all the young men, as well as all the older men who had any weight of judgment or influence, assembled there, but they had also collected in one place all the ships that they had anywhere; and when these were lost, those who survived had no place to retire to, nor any means of defending their towns. Therefore they surrendered themselves and all their possessions to Caesar. He decided that their punishment must be the more severe in order that the rights of ambassadors might be more carefully respected by the natives in the future. He therefore put all their senators to death, and sold all the others into slavery.

CHAPTER 17

WHILE THESE OPERATIONS were going on in the country of the Veneti, Quintus Titurius Sabinus with those forces which he had received from Caesar arrived in the country of the Venelli. Their ruler was Viridovix; he also held the chief command of all those states which had revolted, from which he had raised an army and large forces. And, within a few days after the arrival of Sabinus, the Aulerci, the Eburovices, and the Lexovii slew their senators because they did not favor the war, shut their gates, and united with Viridovix. Moreover, from all over Gaul there had come together a great multitude of desperadoes and bandits whom the hope of plunder and the love of war lured away from farming and daily toil. Sabinus kept himself in his camp, in a spot suitable in all respects, while Viridovix encamped opposite him at a distance of two miles, and daily led out his forces and gave him a chance to fight, so that at last Sabinus not only incurred the contempt of the enemy, but also was criticized rather sharply by the remarks of his own soldiers; and he produced so strong an impression of cowardice that the enemy even dared to come up to the rampart of our camp. Sabinus did this because he did not think that a lieutenant ought to engage in battle with so large a force of the enemy, especially in the absence of his commander-in-chief, except in an advantageous position or when some favorable opportunity presented itself.

CHAPTER 18

AFTER HE HAD ESTABLISHED this impression of cowardice, he selected from his auxiliaries a capable and tactful Gaul and induced him by promises of large rewards to go over to the enemy; he explained to him what he wanted done. When this man came to them as if he were a deserter, he set before them the timidity of the Romans; he pointed out to them by what difficulties Caesar himself was beset by the Veneti, and that, no later than the following night, Sabinus would stealthily lead his army out of his camp and set out to bring aid to Caesar. When they heard this, they all cried out that the chance to score a notable success should not be lost; that they ought to attack the

Roman camp. Many considerations led the Gauls to this decision: the inaction of Sabinus during the preceding days; the assurance of the deserter; their own shortage of food, for which they had carelessly made little provision; the hope arising from the war with the Veneti; and the fact that men as a rule willingly believe what they want to believe. Influenced by these considerations, they did not let Viridovix and the other leaders leave the council until permission had been granted to them to take up arms and hasten to the Roman camp. When this permission had been granted, as if victory were already assured, they joyfully gathered brushwood and fagots, with which to fill up the trenches of the Romans, and advanced to the Roman camp.

CHAPTER 19

THE CAMP WAS SITUATED on high ground, gradually sloping from the bottom for about a mile. To this place the Gauls hastened at full speed, in order that as little time as possible might be given to the Romans to form their lines and to arm, and they were out of breath when they arrived. Having exhorted his men, Sabinus gave them the signal which they were eagerly awaiting. Since the enemy were hampered by the loads which they were carrying, he ordered a sudden sally to be made from two gates. Because of the advantageous position of the camp, the inexperience and exhaustion of the enemy, the valor of our soldiers and their experience in former battles, the result was that the Gauls could not withstand even a single attack of our men, but immediately turned and ran.

Hampered as the enemy were, our men pursued them with their strength unimpaired, and killed a great number of them; our cavalry pursued the rest, and left but a few who had escaped from the fleeing crowd. Thus, at the same time, Sabinus was informed of the naval battle and Caesar of the victory of Sabinus; all the states immediately surrendered to Titurius. For while the Gauls are temperamentally impetuous and ready to undertake war, they are also characteristically yielding and not at all capable of meeting reverses.

CHAPTER 20

ABOUT THE SAME TIME, Publius Crassus arrived in Aquitania, which, as has been said before, constitutes a third district of Gaul. When he saw that he had to wage war in the same localities where a few years before the lieutenant Lucius Valerius Praeconinus had been killed after his army had been routed, and from which the proconsul Lucius Manlius had fled with the loss of his baggage, he realized that he must exercise no ordinary care. Accordingly, he provided a supply of grain, collected auxiliaries and cavalry, and called up individually many brave men from Tolosa, Carcaso, and Narbo, cities in the Province of Gaul close to these regions. Then he led his army into the territory of the Sotiates. When the Sotiates heard of his arrival, they collected large forces, and with their cavalry, in which lay their chief strength, attacked our army on the march, fought their first cavalry battle with our cavalry, then, when their cavalry was routed and pursued by our men, they suddenly uncovered their infantry forces, which they had placed in ambush in a valley. These attacked our scattered men and renewed the fight.

CHAPTER 21

THEY FOUGHT long and fiercely, since the Sotiates, relying on their previous victories, felt that the safety of all Aquitania depended on their courage, while our men wished to show what they could accomplish with a youth as leader, without their general and without the other legions. At length, worn out with wounds, the enemy fled. A large number of them were slain; then Crassus directly after marching began to attack the town of the Sotiates. Since they offered brave resistance, he brought up *vineae* and siege towers. The enemy at one time attempted a sally, at another drove tunnels to our rampart and *vineae*, an operation in which the Aquitani are very experienced, because in many places in their territory there are copper mines and excavations. When they realized that, because of the watchfulness of our men, nothing could be accomplished by these devices, they sent envoys to Crassus and requested him to accept their surrender. Their request was granted; they were ordered to hand over their arms; this they did.

CHAPTER 22

WHILE THE ATTENTION of our soldiers was occupied with these events, Adiatunnus, who held the chief command, tried to make a sally from another part of the town with six hundred faithful followers

whom they call *soldurii*. The terms of their association
are these: In life they enjoy all the privileges in common with those to whose friendship they have devoted
themselves; if anything happens to their comrades
through violence, they either share the same misfortune
at the same time, or commit suicide; and up to this
time no one, within the memory of man, has been found
who, upon the death of the comrade to whose friendship he had devoted himself, refused to die. With these
men Adiatunnus tried to make a sally; but a shout was
raised on that part of the fortification; our men rushed
to arms, and a sharp battle was fought there. Driven
back into the town, Adiatunnus prevailed upon Crassus to grant him his request to enjoy the same terms of
surrender as the rest.

CHAPTER 23

HAVING RECEIVED their arms and hos-
tages, Crassus marched into the territory of the Vocates
and the Tarusates. Then indeed the natives became
alarmed by the report that a town fortified both by its
natural position and by the hand of man had been
taken by storm a few days after our arrival. They
therefore began to send envoys in all directions, to form
alliances, to exchange hostages, and to raise an army.
Envoys were also sent to those states of Hither Spain
which are near Aquitania, summoning auxiliaries and
leaders from them. The arrival of these auxiliaries
made it possible for the natives to enter the war with
an army large in size and in prestige. Those men were
chosen as leaders who had served with Quintus Serto-

rius during all those years, and were considered to have the greatest skill in military affairs. These, following the Roman practice, began to choose locations, to fortify camps, and to cut off our men from supplies. When Crassus realized that his forces by reason of their small number could not easily spread out, whereas the enemy both roamed at will and blocked the roads, and still had enough men left to guard their camp, and that for this reason grain and supplies were less easily brought up to him, and that the numbers of the enemy were increasing day by day, he thought that he ought not to put off fighting a decisive battle. He referred this matter to a council of war, and when he found that all held the same opinion, he set the following day for the battle.

CHAPTER 24

AT DAYBREAK he brought out all his forces and drew them up in a double line; he placed the auxiliaries in the center, and waited to see what plan the enemy would adopt. Although by reason of their great numbers, their past renown in war, and the small numbers of our men the Gauls thought that they could fight with safety, nevertheless they thought it safer to block the roads and to cut off our supplies, and so to gain a bloodless victory. And if, because of the lack of grain, the Romans began to retreat, they planned to attack them on the march while they were encumbered with their packs and dispirited. This plan was approved by their leaders; when the Roman forces were brought out, the Gauls remained in camp. Crassus saw this; and as the enemy by their hesitation and the impression of timidity had made our soldiers more eager to fight, and as the remarks of all the soldiers were heard to the effect that they ought not to delay further to attack the camp, he encouraged his men, and to the delight of his men marched to the enemy's camp.

CHAPTER 25

THERE SOME ROMAN SOLDIERS filled up the trenches, others, by hurling many missiles, dislodged the defenders from the rampart and the fortifications, while the auxiliaries, in whose fighting ability Crassus had little confidence, by bringing up stones and weapons and sods for building a rampart, presented the appearance and impression of combatants. The enemy too were fighting resolutely and boldly, and their missiles, discharged from a higher position, fell not without effect. The cavalry, having ridden about the enemy's camp, reported to Crassus that their camp was not fortified with the same care on the side of the rear gate, and offered an easy access.

CHAPTER 26

CRASSUS EXHORTED the commanders of the cavalry to spur on their men by promises of large rewards, and showed what he wished them to do. Following his orders, the commanders led out those cohorts which had been left to guard the camp and were not worn out by exertion, and led them around by a

somewhat longer detour, so that they might not be seen
from the enemy's camp. While the eyes and minds of
all were intent upon the battle, they quickly reached the
fortifications mentioned above, demolished them, and
established themselves in the enemy's camp before they
could be clearly seen by them, or before it could be
found out what was happening. Then our men, hearing a shout in that direction, began with renewed
strength to fight more fiercely, as generally happens
when there is hope of victory. The enemy, surrounded
on all sides and in utter despair, hastened to throw
themselves down over the fortifications and to seek
safety in flight. Our cavalry pursued them over wide
and open plains; and of fifty thousand men known to
have assembled from Aquitania and the country of the
Cantabri, scarcely a quarter escaped. Late at night the
cavalry returned to camp.

CHAPTER 27

HEARING OF THIS BATTLE, the greatest
part of Aquitania surrendered to Crassus and of its own
accord sent hostages; among them were the Tarbelli,
the Bigerriones, the Ptianii, the Vocates, the Tarusates, the Elusates, the Gates, the Ausci, the Garumni,
the Sibusates, and the Cocosates. A few of the most
distant tribes, relying on the season of the year, as
winter was at hand, neglected to do this.

CHAPTER 28

ABOUT THE SAME TIME, although the summer was almost over, Caesar led his army against the Morini and the Menapii, because, while Gaul as a whole had been subdued, these were the only tribes that remained under arms and had never sent envoys to him to sue for peace; he thought that he could quickly bring that war to an end. But these tribes began to conduct the war in a way far different from that of the rest of the Gauls. For, as they knew that the most powerful tribes which had engaged in battle with Caesar had been routed and vanquished, and as they possessed continuous forests and marshes, they betook themselves with all their possessions there. When Caesar had arrived at the edge of these forests and had begun to fortify his camp, he saw nothing of the enemy. But when our men were working in scattered groups, the enemy suddenly rushed forth from all parts of the forest and attacked them. These quickly took up arms and drove the enemy back into the forests. After slaying a great number of them, they pursued them too far over rather difficult ground and lost a few of their own men.

CHAPTER 29

DURING THE REMAINING DAYS, without interruption, Caesar was busy cutting down the forests; and that no flank attack might be made on the soldiers while they were unarmed and off their guard, he

stacked up opposite the enemy all the timber that was
cut down, and built it up as a rampart on both flanks.
Within a few days a great space was cleared with incredible speed. The enemy's cattle and the rear of their
baggage train were already in our hands, and the men
themselves sought the denser forests. But then such
violent storms arose that the work was necessarily
stopped, and because of the continuation of the rain-
storms the soldiers could no longer remain in their
tents. Therefore, after laying waste all the fields of the
enemy and after setting fire to their villages and buildings, Caesar led his army back and placed it in winter
quarters among the Aulerci, the Lexovii, and the rest of
the states which had recently waged war.

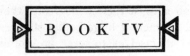

BOOK IV

CHAPTER 1

IN THE FOLLOWING WINTER, when
Gnaeus Pompey and Marcus Crassus were consuls, two
German tribes, the Usipetes and the Tencteri, with a
large number of men crossed the Rhine not far from
the sea into which it flows. They crossed the river because for several years they had been harassed by the
Suebi and hard pressed by them in war and kept from
tilling the soil. The Suebi are by far the largest and
most warlike nation of all the Germans. They are said
to possess a hundred cantons, from each of which they
draw annually a thousand armed men for the purpose
of carrying on war outside their territory. The rest,
who are left at home, support themselves and those
in the field; they again, in turn, are under arms the following year, and the others remain at home. Thus neither the cultivation of the soil nor the pursuit of war in
theory and practice is interrupted. They have, however,
no private or marked-off land, and are not allowed
to remain longer than a year in one place in order to
till the soil. They do not use much grain, but live for
the most part on milk and meat, and devote much time
to hunting. This practice, and the kind of food, their
regular exercise, and the freedom of life (for, accustomed from childhood to no duty or discipline, they do

nothing at all against their will) foster their strength and make them men of huge bodily stature. And they have trained themselves to wear no clothing, except skins, even in the coldest places, and these skins are so scanty that a great part of the body is left bare; they bathe in the rivers.

CHAPTER 2

THEY ALLOW TRADERS access to them so that they may have persons to whom they may sell the booty which they have taken in war rather than because they desire the importation of any commodity. Moreover, the Germans do not import horses, animals which afford the Gauls the keenest pleasure, and which they obtain at great expense, but by regular training they render the small and ugly native animals capable of the greatest endurance. In cavalry combats they often leap from their horses and fight on foot, and they train their horses to remain on the same spot where they have been left, and they get back quickly to them when necessary; in their judgment, nothing is regarded more disgraceful or more unmanly than the use of saddles. And so, however few they may be, they have the courage to advance against any number of cavalry using saddles. They do not at all permit the importation of wine, because they believe that men lose their vigor and become effeminate by its use.

CHAPTER 3

THEY CONSIDER IT the greatest glory of a nation to keep the largest possible area on its borders unoccupied; for this, they think, is definite proof that a great number of states cannot withstand their power. Thus, on one side of the Suebi the country is said to be uninhabited for about one hundred miles. On the opposite side their neighbors are the Ubii, whose state was once large and prosperous by German standards. They are somewhat more civilized than the other tribes of the same race because their borders touch the Rhine and traders visit them frequently, and because of their proximity to the Gauls they have become familiar with their customs. Although the Suebi had tried in frequent wars to drive them from their territory, they could not do so because of the extent of their state and their power of resistance; but they made them pay tribute, and caused them to become much less prominent and powerful.

CHAPTER 4

IN THE SAME PLIGHT were the above-mentioned Usipetes and Tencteri. For many years they withstood the force of the Suebi; but finally they were driven from their territory, and after wandering for three years over many parts of Germany, they came to the Rhine, to the districts which the Menapii inhabited. These possessed lands, buildings, and villages on both banks of the river; but alarmed by the arrival of so great a multitude, they left the buildings which they had across the river, and, having stationed garrisons on this side of the Rhine, they tried to prevent the Germans from crossing. The Germans tried every expedient, but they could neither force a passage because of their lack of boats, nor cross secretly because of the guards of the Menapii. They therefore pretended that they were returning to their own homes and districts. After a march of three days they returned; their cavalry covered the entire distance in a single night and surprised the Menapii who were ignorant of the activity of the Germans and so off their guard. The Menapii, having been informed by their scouts of the departure of the Germans, without fear had moved back to the east side of the Rhine into their own villages. The Germans killed them and seized their boats; they then crossed the river before that part of the Menapii who lived on the near side of the Rhine could be informed of what was happening; then, seizing all their buildings, they lived off their supplies during the rest of the winter.

CHAPTER 5

CAESAR WAS INFORMED of these events; as he feared the fickleness of the Gauls because they are irresponsible in forming plans and for the most part are eager for a change of government, he thought that no reliance whatever ought to be placed on them. For it is a habit of the Gauls to stop travelers, even against their will, and to inquire what each of them may have heard or learned about any matter; and in the towns the common people gather round traders, and compel them to declare from what districts they have come and what they have learned there. Induced by these reports and mere hearsay, they often form plans of the utmost importance, of which they must necessarily immediately afterwards repent, since they are the slaves of indefinite rumors, and since most men when questioned make up answers to gratify them.

CHAPTER 6

AS CAESAR WAS AWARE of their habit, in order that he might not have to face too serious a war, he set out to join his army earlier than was his custom. When he arrived there, he learned that what he suspected would take place had taken place; embassies had been sent by some states to the Germans, requesting them to leave the Rhine; they promised that everything which the Germans demanded would be furnished by them. Influenced by this prospect, the Germans now roamed about more widely, and they had reached the territory of the Eburones and that of the Condrusi, dependents of the Treveri. Having summoned the leading men of Gaul, Caesar thought that he ought to keep secret the information which he had obtained; he soothed and encouraged them, and, having raised some cavalry, he announced his intention of making war on the Germans.

CHAPTER 7

HAVING PROVIDED A SUPPLY of grain and selected his cavalry, he began to march towards those districts in which he heard the Germans were. When he was a few days' march from them, envoys came from them, whose plea was as follows: The Germans did not take the lead in making war upon the Roman people, but if provoked, they would not refuse to fight; for it was the custom of the Germans, handed down to them by their ancestors, to resist those who made war upon them, and not to beg for mercy. They declared, however, that they had come to Gaul against their will, because they had been driven forth from their homes. If the Romans would have their good will, they could be their useful friends. Let the Romans either assign them lands, or allow them to keep those which they had acquired by arms. They admitted their inferiority to the Suebi alone, to whom even the immortal gods could not be a match; there was no one else on earth whom they could not conquer.

CHAPTER 8

TO THIS PLEA Caesar replied as seemed proper; but the conclusion of his speech was as follows: He could have no friendly relations with them if they remained in Gaul. It was not right that those who could not defend their own territory should seize that of others; nor were there in Gaul any fields lying unoccupied which could be given away justly, especially to so great a number of men; but they could, if they

wished, settle in the territory of the Ubii, whose envoys were with him, complaining of the wrongs done
them by the Suebi and seeking his assistance; he
would order the Ubii to allow them to do this.

CHAPTER 9

THE ENVOYS SAID that they would re-
port this to their people and, after deliberation upon
the matter, would return to Caesar in three days; they
asked him not to move his camp nearer to them in
the meantime. Caesar said that he could not grant
them this request either. For he knew that some days
before they had sent a large part of their cavalry across
the Meuse to the territory of the Ambivariti, to get
booty and forage; he thought that they were waiting
for this cavalry and for that reason were anxious for a
delay.

CHAPTER 10

THE MEUSE RISES in the Vosges moun-
tains, which are in the country of the Lingones, and,
receiving from the Rhine a tributary called the Waal,
it forms with this the island of the Batavi, and not
more than eighty miles from there it flows into the
Ocean. The Rhine, moreover, rises in the country of the
Lepontii, who inhabit the Alps, and in a long course
flows rapidly through the territories of the Nantuates,
the Helvetii, the Sequani, the Mediomatrici, the Triboci, and the Treveri; where it approaches the Ocean,

it divides into several branches, forming many large islands. Many of these are inhabited by wild savage tribes, some of whom are believed to live on fish and birds' eggs. It flows into the Ocean by many mouths.

CHAPTER 11

WHEN CAESAR was not more than twelve miles from the enemy, their envoys returned to him, as had been agreed; meeting him on the march, they earnestly pleaded with him not to advance farther. When their request was denied, they asked him to send word to the cavalry in advance of the army, forbidding them to engage in battle, and to give them permission to send envoys to the Ubii. They declared that if the leading men and the senate of the Ubii would give them an oath-bound pledge of good faith, they would accept the terms proposed by Caesar, and asked that Caesar give them three days to settle these matters. Caesar thought that all these pleas had the same end in view—to secure a delay of three days so that their absent cavalry might return. However, he said that on that day he would not advance farther than four miles, in order to get water. He ordered them to assemble on the following day in that place with as many of their men as possible in order that he might inquire into their demands. Meanwhile, he sent messengers to the commanders who had gone ahead with all the cavalry to convey the order not to attack the enemy, and, if they themselves were attacked, to sustain the attack until he himself came up nearer with the army.

CHAPTER 12

BUT AS SOON AS THE ENEMY saw our
cavalry, which numbered five thousand, although they
themselves had no more than eight hundred horsemen,
because those men who had gone across the Meuse to
get grain had not yet returned, they charged our men
and speedily threw them into disorder. Our men
thought that they had nothing to fear, as the envoys of
the Germans had left Caesar but a short while before,
and had requested a truce for that day. When they
again offered resistance, the enemy, according to their
custom, leaped to the ground, and, stabbing our horses
underneath, unseated quite a number of our men, put
the rest to flight, and drove them forward in such a
panic that our men did not stop fleeing until they came
in sight of our marching column. In that engagement
seventy-four of our cavalry were slain, among them
the Aquitanian Piso, a very brave man, descended
from a very distinguished family, whose grandfather
had held the sovereignty in his own state, and had
been called "Friend" by the Roman Senate. When he
was bringing assistance to his brother, who had been
cut off by the enemy, he rescued him from danger;
but he himself was thrown down from his horse, which
was wounded; he resisted most bravely as long as he
could. When he was surrounded, and fell after receiving many wounds, his brother, who had escaped
from the fight, saw from a distance what had happened;
spurring on his horse, he hurled himself upon the
enemy, and was slain.

CHAPTER 13

AFTER THIS BATTLE, Caesar thought that he ought not to give an audience to their envoys, nor to accept terms from those who, after suing for peace, had craftily and treacherously made an attack without provocation. Moreover, he judged it the height of folly to wait till the enemy's forces should be increased and their cavalry should return. Knowing the fickleness of the Gauls, he realized how much prestige the Germans had already gained among them by a single engagement. Therefore he thought that no time ought to be given them for the formation of further plans. Having reached this decision, he imparted to his lieutenants and quaestor his determination not to let slip any chance to fight. Then a most favorable event occurred. Early next morning, prepared to practice the same treachery and deceit, a large company of Germans, comprising all the leading men and elders, came to Caesar's camp. Their ostensible object was to apologize for starting the battle the day before contrary to the agreement they themselves had requested. At the same time, if in any degree possible, they intended by playing false to prevail upon Caesar to grant them an extension of the truce. Caesar was delighted that they had fallen into his hands, and ordered them to be detained; he then led all his forces out of camp, and ordered the cavalry to follow in the rear, because he thought they were upset by the recent engagement.

CHAPTER 14

CAESAR DREW UP HIS ARMY in a triple line and quickly made a march of eight miles. He reached the camp of the enemy before the Germans could sense what was happening. They suddenly became panic-stricken by everything, both by the speed of our advance and by the absence of their leaders. As no time was given them to form a plan or take up arms, they were too confused to be able to decide whether it was best to lead their forces against the enemy, to defend the camp, or to seek safety in flight. When their fear was betrayed by the uproar and tumult, our soldiers, enraged by their treachery of the previous day, burst into the camp. There those who could speedily take up arms resisted our men for a while, and fought amidst the carts and baggage trains; but the rest of the crowd, consisting of women and children (for they had departed from home and crossed the Rhine with all their families), began to flee in all directions; Caesar sent the cavalry to hunt them down.

CHAPTER 15

HEARING THE SHRIEKS in the rear and seeing their own families slain, the Germans threw down their arms, deserted their standards, and rushed out of the camp. When they had reached the confluence of the Meuse and the Rhine, they abandoned hope of further flight. A great number of them were slain, and the rest hurled themselves into the river and there perished, overcome by fear, weariness, and the force of the current. Our men returned to camp, safe to a man, with only a few wounded, notwithstanding their apprehension of a hard campaign, since the number of the enemy amounted to 430,000. Caesar gave those whom he had detained in camp permission to depart. But they, fearing punishment and torture at the hands of the Gauls, whose lands they had laid waste, said that they wished to remain with him. Caesar granted them leave to stay.

CHAPTER 16

UPON THE CONCLUSION of the German campaign Caesar decided that he ought to cross the Rhine for many reasons; of these the strongest was that, since he saw that the Germans were so easily induced to come into Gaul, he wanted them to fear for their own interests also, when they realized that a Roman army both could and dared cross the Rhine. There was the further reason that the cavalry division of the Usipetes and the Tencteri, which, as I have mentioned above, had crossed the Meuse for the purpose of plundering and obtaining forage, and had taken no part in the battle, after the flight of their countrymen had withdrawn across the Rhine into the territory of the Sugambri and united with them. When Caesar had sent envoys to the Sugambri to demand the surrender of those who had made war upon him and on Gaul, they replied that the Rhine marked the limit of Roman sovereignty; if he did not think it right that the Germans should cross into Gaul against his will, why

should he claim that anything beyond the Rhine was
under his authority or power? Moreover, the Ubii, who
alone of the peoples across the Rhine had sent envoys
to Caesar, had formed an alliance, and given hostages,
earnestly begged him to aid them, because they were
grievously hard pressed by the Suebi; or, if he was
prevented from doing that by the requirements of public business, they asked him at least to transport his
army across the Rhine; that movement would be enough
for their present help and give them hope for the future.
For, they said, in consequence of the defeat of Ariovistus and the success of this latest battle, so great was
the name and reputation of his army, even among the
farthest tribes of the Germans, that they would be safe
because of the prestige and friendship of the Roman
people. They promised a large number of boats for
transporting the army.

CHAPTER 17

FOR THE REASONS mentioned above
Caesar had decided to cross the Rhine; but he did not
consider it sufficiently safe or consistent with his own
prestige or that of the Roman people to cross in boats.
And so, although there was the greatest difficulty in
building a bridge on account of the breadth, the swift-
ness, and the depth of the river, nevertheless he
thought that he ought to make every effort to do this,
or else not lead his army across. The plan of the
bridge which he devised was as follows: He fastened
together, two feet apart, a pair of logs, each a foot and
a half thick, sharpened slightly at the lower end,

their length determined by the depth of the river. These he lowered into the river by means of mechanical appliances, planted them firmly, and drove them home with piledrivers, not perpendicularly, as piles are usually driven in, but leaning forward with a decided slant, so that they inclined in the direction of the current. Opposite these at a distance of forty feet on the lower side he placed two piles, fastened together in the same manner, slanting forward against the violent onrush of the current. These two pairs of piles were held apart by a pair of braces on each side at the very end, after a beam having the thickness of two feet, corresponding with the space between the piles, had been let in. Now that these two pairs of piles were held apart and clamped together in opposite directions, so great was the stability of the structure and such its character that the greater the force of the water rushing against it, the more closely they were tied and held together. These piers were joined by timber laid over them in the direction of the bridge, and were covered with long poles and wickerwork; furthermore, piles were driven with a slant into the water, on the downstream side, in order that they, set below as props and connected with the whole structure, might withstand the force of the stream; other piles likewise were placed at a short distance above the bridge, so that, if trunks of trees were floated, or boats were launched by the enemy to break down the structure, their force might be weakened by these defenses, and the bridge might not be damaged.

CHAPTER 18

THE WHOLE WORK was completed within ten days after the timber had begun to be collected, and the army was led across. Caesar left a strong guard at either end of the bridge, and hastened into the territory of the Sugambri. In the meantime, envoys came to him from several states; to their request for peace and friendship he returned a gracious answer, and ordered hostages to be brought to him. But the Sugambri, immediately after the construction of the bridge, taking to flight at the instigation of those of the Tencteri and Usipetes whom they had with them, had left their territory, had carried off all their possessions, and had hidden in the recesses of the forests.

CHAPTER 19

CAESAR REMAINED a few days in their territory, burned all their villages and buildings, cut down the standing grain, and withdrew into the territory of the Ubii; he promised them his assistance if they should be hard pressed by the Suebi, and received the following information from them: After the Suebi had found out through scouts that a bridge was being built, according to their custom they called a council, and sent messengers in all directions, directing the people to leave their towns and to place their children, wives, and all their possessions in the forests; they ordered all those who could bear arms to assemble in one place, almost exactly in the center of those regions

which the Suebi occupied; here they had determined
to await the arrival of the Romans and to fight a decisive battle at that point. When Caesar received this
information, as he had accomplished all the objects for
which he had determined to lead his army across the
Rhine—to strike fear into the Germans, to take vengeance on the Sugambri, and to free the Ubii from op-
pression, and as he had spent altogether eighteen days
across the Rhine, he thought that he had done enough
to satisfy honor and interest, and so he withdrew into
Gaul, and destroyed the bridge.

CHAPTER 20

ONLY A SMALL PART of summer re-
mained; although winter comes early in these regions,
because all Gaul lies towards the north, nevertheless
Caesar determined to invade Britain, because he knew
that in almost all the wars with the Gauls, assistance
had been furnished to our enemy from that country.
Moreover, even if the season of the year was insuffi-
cient for carrying on war, he thought it would be of
great advantage to him if he only visited the island,
observed the character of the people, and became familiar with the localities, the harbors, and the approaches; for nearly all these matters were unknown
to the Gauls. For no one, except traders, goes there
without good reason; and even they know nothing except the seacoast and the districts opposite Gaul. Therefore, he summoned traders from all parts, but he
could not learn from them what was the size of the island, or what tribes or how many inhabited it, what

methods of warfare they employed, what were their
customs, or what harbors were suitable for a large
number of ships.

CHAPTER 21

TO LEARN THESE PARTICULARS before
making the attempt to invade the island, Caesar
thought that Gaius Volusenus was a suitable person to
send ahead with a warship. He ordered him to spy out
everything and to return to him as soon as possible. He
himself set out with all his forces to the territory of the
Morini, because from that country there was the short-
est passage across to Britain. He ordered ships from
all the neighboring districts and the fleet which he had
built the previous summer for the war with the Veneti
to assemble at this place. Meanwhile, since his plan
had been discovered and reported by traders to the
Britons, envoys came to him from several states of the
island to promise that they would give hostages and
that they would submit to the authority of the Roman
people. He gave them an audience, made them a gener-
ous promise, and exhorted them to keep their word;
then he sent them back home, and together with them
he sent Commius, whom, after the defeat of the
Atrebates, he had made king there, a man whose
energy and discretion he appreciated, who, he thought,
was loyal to him, and whose influence was considered
great in those countries. He commanded him to visit all
the states he could, to exhort them to place their confidence in the Roman people, and to inform them that
Caesar would shortly come there. After Volusenus had

surveyed all the localities as far as opportunity allowed a man who did not dare to disembark and trust himself to the natives, he returned to Caesar on the fifth day and reported what he had observed there.

CHAPTER 22

WHILE CAESAR REMAINED in these places for the purpose of fitting out his ships, envoys came to him from a large section of the Morini to apologize for their conduct the previous season, because being uncivilized and unacquainted with our usages they had made war upon the Roman people, and to promise that they would carry out his commands. Caesar thought that this had happened most opportunely, since he did not wish to leave an enemy in the rear; besides, because of the lateness of the season he could not very well start another war, and he judged that the exactions of such trifling matters ought not to have precedence over the invasion of Britain. He therefore ordered them to furnish a large number of hostages, and when these were delivered, he took the Morini under his protection. When about eighty transports (as many as he thought would be enough to carry two legions across) had been pressed into service and brought together, he assigned the warships which he had to the quaestor, the lieutenants, and the subsidiary officers. In addition to this number there were eighteen transports, which were detained eight miles off by the wind so that they were unable to reach the same port; these he assigned to the cavalry. The rest of the army he assigned to the lieutenants Quintus

Titurius Sabinus and Lucius Aurunculeius Cotta for
operations against the Menapii and those cantons of
the Morini from which envoys had not come to him;
he ordered the lieutenant Publius Sulpicius Rufus to
hold the port with a force he thought large enough for
that purpose.

CHAPTER 23

WHEN CAESAR HAD MADE these ar-
rangements and found the weather suitable for sailing,
he set sail about the third watch, and ordered the
cavalry to proceed to the farther port, to embark, and
to follow him. They carried out these orders somewhat
slowly; he himself reached Britain with the first ships
about the fourth hour of the day, and there beheld the
armed forces of the enemy arrayed on all the cliffs.
Such was the nature of the ground, and the sea was so
closely bordered by abrupt cliffs that a missile could
be hurled from the higher places upon the shore. Considering this place by no means suitable for disembarking, he waited at anchor till the ninth hour for the
rest of the ships to assemble there. In the meantime,
he summoned the lieutenants and the military tribunes, and told them both what he had learned from
Volusenus and what he wished to be done. He warned
them as military practice—above all, as marine service
—required, since these are subject to rapid and con-
stant change, that all orders be carried out by them
instantly and at the right time. He then dismissed
them, and securing both favorable wind and tide, he
gave the signal, weighed anchor, advanced about

seven miles from that spot, and ran the ships aground
on an open and level shore.

CHAPTER 24

THE NATIVES, realizing the intention of
the Romans, sent forward their cavalry and chariot-
fighters, a type of warrior which they regularly employ
in battle, and following with the rest of their forces,
tried to prevent our men from disembarking. For
the following reasons our men found disembarkation
very difficult: Our ships, on account of their size, could
not be grounded, except in deep water; moreover, our
soldiers, being on unfamiliar ground, their hands
encumbered, weighed down by the large and heavy
burden of arms, had at one and the same time to leap
down from the ships, to stand in the midst of the waves,
and to fight with the enemy, while the Britons, either
from dry land or advancing a little way into the water,
with all their limbs free, and thoroughly acquainted
with the ground, boldly hurled their weapons, and
spurred on their trained horses. Our men, frightened
by all this and wholly inexperienced in this sort of
fighting, did not display the same enthusiasm and
eagerness as they were accustomed to display in engagements on dry land.

CHAPTER 25

WHEN CAESAR NOTICED THIS, he or-
dered the warships, whose appearance was less familiar to the enemy and whose movement was more easily
controlled, to be removed a little from the transports,

to be driven forward with oars, and to moor on the exposed flank of the enemy, and from there to beat back and drive away the enemy with slings, arrows, and artillery; this manoeuver was highly advantageous to our forces. For the natives, frightened by the shape of our ships, the motion of the oars, and the strange type of artillery, halted and retreated just a little. And now, while our men were hesitating, chiefly because of the depth of the sea, the eaglebearer of the Tenth Legion, after praying to the gods that his action might turn out favorably for the legion, cried: "Leap down, fellow-soldiers, unless you wish to betray your eagle to the enemy; I, at any rate, shall do my duty to my country and my general." When he had said this in a loud voice, he leaped from the ship, and began to bear the eagle against the enemy. Then our men, exhorting one another not to disgrace themselves by the loss of the eagle, leaped from the ship in a body. When the men on the nearest ship saw them, they followed them, and advanced against the enemy.

CHAPTER 26

THERE WAS SHARP FIGHTING on both sides. Our men, however, were thrown into great disorder because they could neither keep ranks, nor get a firm footing, nor follow their standards, and because men from different ships attached themselves to any standards that they had fallen in with; the enemy, on the other hand, knew all the shallows, and whenever from the shore they saw several men disembarking one by one from a ship, spurring on their horses, they would attack them while they were at a disadvantage, many of them surrounding a few of our men, while others hurled weapons upon our groups of soldiers on the exposed flank. When Caesar had noticed this, he ordered the small boats of the warships and the scouting vessels to be manned with soldiers, and he sent them to aid those whom he had observed to be in difficulty. As soon as our men stood firm on dry ground and all their comrades joined them, they made an attack on the enemy and put them to flight; but they could not pursue them too far, because the cavalry transports had not been able to hold their course and to make the island. That was the only thing that prevented Caesar from enjoying his usual good fortune.

CHAPTER 27

AS SOON AS THE ENEMY, overcome in battle, recovered from their flight, they at once sent envoys to Caesar to ask for peace; they promised to give hostages and do what he commanded. Together with these envoys came the Atrebatian Commius, who, I had stated above, had been sent ahead by Caesar into Britain. When he had disembarked, although he was bringing Caesar's message to them in the character of an envoy, he was arrested and thrown into chains by the Britons; now, after the battle, they sent him back. In asking for peace they laid the blame for that act upon the common people, and asked that they be pardoned because of their ignorance. Caesar complained that, after they had voluntarily sent envoys to the continent and had sought peace from him, they had made war on him without cause; but he said that he would pardon their ignorance, and demanded hostages. Some of these they gave at once; others, they said, would be delivered in a few days, after they had been summoned from more distant places. Meanwhile they ordered their people to return to their fields, and the leading men began to assemble from all quarters, and to put themselves and their states under Caesar's protection.

CHAPTER 28

PEACE WAS ESTABLISHED by these measures. Three days after our arrival in Britain, the eighteen ships, mentioned above, which had taken the cavalry on board, sailed from the upper port with a light breeze. When these were approaching Britain and were visible from the camp, suddenly so great a storm sprang up that none of them could hold its course; some were driven back to the same port from which they had sailed, while others were driven with great danger to themselves to the lower part of the island, which is nearer the west; nevertheless they anchored, but when they were filling with water, they were forced to put out to sea in the face of the night, and made for the continent.

CHAPTER 29

THAT NIGHT there happened to be a full moon, and this date usually causes very high tides in the Ocean, and that fact was unknown to our men. And so, at one and the same time, the tide filled the warships in which Caesar had had the army brought over, and which he had hauled up on dry land, and the storm shattered the transports which were riding at anchor, and our men were given no opportunity of managing the vessels or rendering aid. Many ships were wrecked, and since the rest, on account of the loss of their cables, anchors, and the remainder of their rigging, were useless for sailing, a great commotion, as was bound to happen, arose throughout the army. For there were no other ships to carry the men back, and everything necessary for repairing ships was lacking, and since it was clear to all that they would have to winter in Gaul, no grain had been provided in Britain for the winter.

CHAPTER 30

ON LEARNING of these things, the leading men of Britain, who had assembled at Caesar's headquarters after the battle, held a conference. Since they understood that the Romans lacked cavalry, ships and grain, and since they supposed that our soldiers were few in number because of the small size of the camp (which was even smaller than usual because Caesar had brought the legions over without heavy baggage), they decided that the best thing to do was to renew hostilities, to cut off our men from grain and provisions, and to prolong their operations into the winter; for they were confident that if these invaders were vanquished or cut off from returning, no one in the future would cross over into Britain to make war. Therefore, they again formed a conspiracy, and began to depart from the camp a few at a time, and secretly to bring up their men from the fields.

CHAPTER 31

ALTHOUGH CAESAR was not yet familiar with their plans, yet from what had happened to his ships and from the fact that they had stopped sending hostages, he suspected that that would happen which actually did happen. Therefore, he provided for every emergency. He collected grain daily from the fields into the camp, and he used the timber and bronze of the ships which had been most seriously damaged to repair the others, and ordered whatever else was necessary for that purpose to be brought from the continent. And so, since the work was carried on by the soldiers with the utmost enthusiasm, although twelve ships had been lost, Caesar made it possible to use the rest fairly well for sailing.

CHAPTER 32

WHILE THIS WAS GOING ON, one legion, called the Seventh, was sent as usual to get grain. Up to that time no suspicion of hostilities had arisen, since part of the Britons remained in the fields, and others came frequently to the camp. Then those who were on guard at the gates of the camp reported to Caesar that a greater cloud of dust than usual was seen in that direction in which the legion had marched. Suspecting that which was actually the case, namely, that some new scheme had been worked up by the natives, Caesar ordered the cohorts which were on guard to proceed with him in that direction, two of the others to relieve them, and the rest to arm and to follow him with all haste. When he had advanced some little distance from the camp, he saw that his men were being hard pressed by the enemy and were holding their own with difficulty, and since the legion was crowded together, missiles were hurled upon them from all sides. For since the grain had all been cut from the rest of the fields, and only one part remained, the enemy, suspecting that our men would come there, had hidden during the night in the woods. Then, when our men, having laid aside their weapons, were scattered and busy reaping, they made a sudden attack on them, killed a few, threw the rest into confusion, since their ranks were in disorder, and at the same time surrounded them with cavalry and war chariots.

CHAPTER 33

THEIR METHOD OF FIGHTING from chariots is as follows: First of all they drive about in all directions and hurl missiles, and by the mere fright caused by the horses and by the noise of the wheels they generally throw the ranks of the enemy into confusion; and when they have worked their way through the squadrons of their own cavalry, they leap down from the chariots and fight on foot. Meanwhile the charioteers withdraw gradually from the battle and place the chariots in such a way that, if the chariot-fighters are hard pressed by a large number of

the enemy, they have a convenient retreat to their own
lines. Thus they exhibit in battle the speed of cavalry
and the steadiness of infantry; and by daily practice
and exercise they become so expert that even on a sloping and steep place they are accustomed to keep control of their horses at full speed, to check them and
turn them in a moment, to run along the pole, stand
on the yoke, and from there to return to their chariots
with the utmost speed.

CHAPTER 34

WHEN OUR MEN were greatly disturbed
by these tactics and the strange character of the fighting, Caesar brought them assistance at the right moment; for upon his arrival the enemy halted, and our
men recovered from their fear. Though this had been
accomplished, he thought that the time was unfavorable for attacking the enemy and for joining battle; he
therefore kept himself on ground favorable to himself,
and after a short interval he led the legions back to
camp. While this was going on, and all our men were
fully occupied, the natives who remained in the fields
withdrew. Then for several days in succession there
followed storms which kept our men in camp and
prevented the enemy from fighting. Meanwhile the
Britons dispatched messengers in all directions and
reported to their people the small number of our soldiers, and pointed out how great a chance they had
of securing booty and of freeing themselves forever, if
they could drive the Romans from their camp. In this
way they quickly assembled a large number of infantry and cavalry and advanced towards our camp.

CHAPTER 35

ALTHOUGH CAESAR SAW that the same thing which had happened on previous occasions would happen again, that the enemy, if routed, would escape from danger by their speed, nevertheless, having obtained about thirty horsemen, whom the Atrebatian Commius, of whom mention has been made above, had brought over with him, he drew up the legions in line of battle before the camp. When the battle was joined, the enemy were unable to withstand the attack of our soldiers very long and fled. Our men pursued them as far as their speed and strength allowed, and killed a great number of them; then, after setting fire to all their buildings far and wide, they returned to their camp.

CHAPTER 36

ON THE SAME DAY envoys sent by the enemy came to Caesar to sue for peace. For them Caesar doubled the number of hostages he had previously demanded, and ordered them to be brought to the continent, because the season of the equinox was near at hand, and he did not think it right that damaged ships should run the risk of sailing in stormy weather. Having secured favorable weather, he set sail a little after midnight; all the ships reached the continent safely, but two transports could not make the same port as the rest and were carried a little lower down the coast.

CHAPTER 37

WHEN ABOUT three hundred soldiers had disembarked from these two transports and were hastening to the camp, the Morini, whom Caesar had left in a state of peace when he was setting out for Britain, were induced by the hope of booty and surrounded them, at first with a not very large number of men, and ordered them to lay down their arms if they did not wish to be killed. When our soldiers formed a circle and were defending themselves, on hearing the uproar about six thousand of the enemy quickly assembled. When this was reported, Caesar sent the whole of the cavalry from the camp to aid his men. Meanwhile our soldiers withstood the attack of the enemy, and fought very bravely for more than four hours; they received but few wounds, and killed many of the enemy. But after our cavalry came into sight, the enemy threw down their arms and fled, and a great number of them were killed.

CHAPTER 38

THE NEXT DAY Caesar sent the lieutenant Titus Labienus with those legions which he had brought back from Britain against the Morini, who had renewed hostilities. And since they had no place to which they might escape on account of the dryness of the marshes (the refuge of which they had availed themselves in the previous year), almost all of them came into the power of Labienus. However, the lieu-

tenants Quintus Titurius and Lucius Cotta, who had
led the legions into the territory of the Menapii, laid
waste all their fields, cut down their grain, and burned
their buildings, because the Menapii had all hidden in
their deepest forests; they then returned to Caesar.
Caesar established the winter quarters of all the legions among the Belgae. Only two British states sent
hostages there; the rest neglected to do so. Upon receipt of Caesar's dispatches, a thanksgiving of
twenty days was decreed by the Senate for these
achievements.

BOOK V

CHAPTER 1

IN THE CONSULSHIP of Lucius Domitius and Appius Claudius, when Caesar was on the point of departing from his winter quarters for Italy, as he was accustomed to do each year, he ordered the lieutenants whom he had placed in command of the legions to have as many ships as possible built during the winter and the old ones repaired. He set forth the plan and shape of these ships. For speed of loading and beaching, he had them made a little shallower than those which we are accustomed to use in the Mediterranean, and the more so on this account, because he had found out that because of the frequent changes of the tide the waves of Gaul were smaller; for the purpose of transporting cargo and a large number of draught-animals he had them made a little wider than those which we use on other seas. He ordered all these vessels to be built for rapid movement, and for this purpose the lowness of their decks contributed much. He ordered all materials that were necessary to equip the ships to be brought from Spain. After he had finished holding court in Cisalpine Gaul, Caesar set out for Illyricum, because he heard that the Pirustae were laying waste by raids the part of the Province nearest them. When he had come there, he levied soldiers upon the states, and ordered them to assemble at a certain place. Hearing of this, the Pirustae sent envoys to tell him that none of those raids had been made on the decision of the state, and they declared that they were ready by every means to make restitution for the damage. After hearing their statement, Caesar demanded hostages, and ordered them to be brought to him on a certain day; unless they did this, he declared that he would make war upon their state. The hostages were delivered on time, as he had ordered, and Caesar appointed commissioners between the states to assess the damages and to fix the penalty.

CHAPTER 2

AFTER SETTLING these matters and closing court, Caesar returned to Cisalpine Gaul, and from there proceeded to the army. When he had come there, he visited all the winter quarters, and found that, in spite of the utmost shortage of all necessary materials, because of their extraordinary energy the soldiers had built about six hundred ships of the type described above and twenty-eight warships, which could be launched in a few days. Having warmly commended the soldiers and those who had been in charge of the work, he pointed out what he wanted done, and ordered all the ships to assemble at Portus Itius, from which he had learned was the easiest passage to Britain, a distance of about thirty miles from the continent; he left as many soldiers as seemed sufficient for this purpose. With four legions in light marching order and eight hundred horsemen he himself set out for the territory of the Treveri, because they neither came to the councils nor submitted to his authority, and were said to be stirring up the Germans beyond the Rhine.

CHAPTER 3

THE STATE OF THE TREVERI has by far the most powerful cavalry in Gaul and great forces of infantry, and, as we have stated above, extends to the Rhine. In that state two men, Indutiomarus and Cingetorix, were rivals for the leadership. As soon as the latter of these learned of the arrival of Caesar and his legions, he came to him and assured him that he and all his followers would remain loyal and not forsake their friendship with the Roman people, and he pointed out what was going on among the Treveri. Indutiomarus, on the other hand, even began to raise cavalry and infantry and to prepare for war, after he had hidden those who by reason of age could not bear arms, in the forest of the Ardennes, which is of immense size and extends through the territory of the Treveri, from the Rhine to the borders of the Remi. But some leading men of that state, influenced by their friendship for Cingetorix, and alarmed by the arrival of our army, came to Caesar and, since they could not look out for the interest of the state, began to plead with him for their own private interests. Now Indutiomarus, fearing that he might be deserted by everybody, sent envoys to Caesar. He declared that on this account he had been reluctant to leave his own people and come to him, because he wished to keep the state more easily in its allegiance, lest, if all the nobles left, the common people might become disloyal through lack of foresight. As a result the state was in his power, and, if Caesar allowed, he would come to his camp and commit his own fortunes and those of the state to his protection.

CHAPTER 4

ALTHOUGH CAESAR KNEW what prompted these remarks, and what circumstances kept him from carrying out the plan which he had formed, nevertheless, in order that he might not be compelled to waste the summer among the Treveri, when everything had been prepared for the campaign in Britain, he ordered Indutiomarus to come to him with two hundred hostages. When these were brought, among them the son of Indutiomarus and all his relatives, whom Caesar had summoned by name, he reassured Indutiomarus and urged him to remain loyal. Nevertheless, summoning to his camp the leading men of the Treveri, he won them over individually to the side of Cingetorix; not only did he understand that he was doing this for what Cingetorix deserved of him, but he also thought that it was of great importance that the influence of one whose singular goodwill towards him he had ascertained should be as strong as possible among his own people. This act offended Indutiomarus greatly; he realized that his influence among his people was being diminished, and although he had previously been ill-disposed towards us, on account of this grievance he became much more indignant.

CHAPTER 5

WHEN THESE MATTERS had been settled, Caesar proceeded with the legions to Portus Itius. There he learned that sixty ships which had been built in the country of the Meldi had been driven back by a storm, had been unable to maintain their course, and had returned to the same port from which they had set out. The rest he found ready for sailing and fully equipped. Cavalry from all Gaul, numbering four thousand, and the leading men from all the states assembled at the same place. Caesar had decided to leave in Gaul only very few of these, whose loyalty towards himself he had ascertained, and to take the rest with him as hostages, because he feared an uprising in Gaul during his absence.

CHAPTER 6

AMONG THE LEADERS was the Aeduan Dumnorix, of whom we have made previous mention. This man in particular Caesar had determined to keep with him, because he knew him to be eager for a revolution, eager for power, a man of great courage and of great influence among the Gauls. Moreover, in an assembly of the Aedui Dumnorix had said that Caesar intended to confer upon him the kingship of the state; the Aedui greatly resented this statement, yet did not dare to send envoys to Caesar either to offer objections or to deprecate his intention. Caesar had learned this fact from his friends. Dumnorix at first

strove by every kind of entreaty to obtain permission
to remain in Gaul, saying that, being unused to sailing, he feared the sea, and also that he was prevented from sailing by religious scruples. After he
saw that his request was firmly refused and that all
hope of obtaining it was lost, he began to stir up the
Gallic leaders, to call them aside one by one, and to
urge them to remain on the continent. He also worked
upon their fears, saying that it was not without reason
that Gaul was being stripped of all her nobility; that
it was Caesar's design to transport to Britain and there
put to death all those whom he feared to kill in the
sight of the Gauls. He pledged his own word to the
rest, and demanded of them an oath that they would
carry out by common consent whatever they judged to
be in the interest of Gaul. These plots were reported to
Caesar by several persons.

CHAPTER 7

WHEN CAESAR RECEIVED this informa-
tion, because he had very high regard for the Aeduan
state, he decided that Dumnorix should be restrained
and deterred by all possible means; and, as he perceived that his madness was going too far, he decided
that he ought to see to it that he should not do any
harm to him personally and to the Roman state. Therefore, while waiting about twenty-five days in that
place, because the northwest wind, which is prevalent
a great part of every season in those places, prevented
his sailing, he was taking pains to keep Dumnorix on
his good behavior, but at the same time to learn all his

plans; having at length secured fair weather, he ordered the soldiers and the cavalry to embark. While all the men were occupied with this operation, Dumnorix together with the cavalry of the Aedui began to leave camp without Caesar's knowledge and to depart for home. When this was reported to Caesar, he put off his departure and laying everything else aside, sent a strong detachment of cavalry to pursue him and bring him back; if he resisted and refused to obey, he ordered him to be put to death; for he thought that Dumnorix, who disregarded his authority to his face, would not behave like a man in his senses while he was absent. When Dumnorix was called back, he began to resist and to defend himself by force, to implore the aid of his followers, crying out repeatedly that he was a free man and a citizen of a free state. Our men, as they were ordered, surrounded the man and killed him; but all the Aeduan cavalry returned to Caesar.

CHAPTER 8

WHEN THIS WAS DONE, Caesar left Labienus on the continent with three legions and two thousand horsemen, to guard the ports, to look out for the grain supply, to learn what was going on in Gaul, and to form such plans as conditions at the time might require. He himself set sail at sunset with five legions and the same number of cavalry as he had left on the continent. He started with a gentle southwest wind, but about midnight the wind failed, and he could not keep his course. He was carried too far by the tide, and at sunrise he caught sight of Britain left behind on the left. Then, again following the change of the tide, he tried by rowing to reach that part of the island where, as he had learned the previous summer, was the best place to land. And in this attempt the spirit of the soldiers was very praiseworthy; in the transports and heavy ships, without interrupting hard rowing, they kept up the speed of the warships. About midday Caesar reached Britain with all the ships, but no enemy was seen in that place. As Caesar afterwards learned from prisoners, large numbers of Britons had assembled there, but alarmed by the large number of our ships, which together with the ships of the previous year and the private vessels which individuals had built for their own convenience numbered more than eight hundred, they had withdrawn from the shore when these were seen at one time, and had hidden on higher ground.

CHAPTER 9

THE ARMY DISEMBARKED and chose a suitable place for the camp. When Caesar learned from prisoners where the forces of the enemy had encamped, he left ten cohorts and three hundred horsemen near the sea to guard the ships and set out against the enemy during the third watch. He was not worried about the ships because he was leaving them at anchor upon a smooth and open shore; he placed Quintus Atrius in command of that guard and the ships. He himself, advancing about twelve miles during the night, caught sight of the enemy's forces. These advanced to the river with their cavalry and chariots, and from the higher ground began to check our men and to engage them in battle. Driven back by our cavalry, they hid in the woods; there they had secured a place remarkably well fortified by nature and art, which, as it seemed, they had prepared before for a civil war, for all the entrances were obstructed by a great number of trees that had been felled. They themselves made sorties out of the woods in small groups, and tried to prevent our men from entering their fortifications. But the soldiers of the Seventh Legion, having formed a *testudo* and thrown up a rampart against the fortifications, captured the place, and drove the enemy out of the woods, having themselves received a few wounds. But Caesar forbade his men to pursue the fleeing enemy too far, both because he did not know the character of the ground, and because a great part of the day had already been spent, and he wished to leave time for the fortification of the camp.

CHAPTER 10

EARLY NEXT MORNING Caesar sent his foot soldiers and cavalry in three divisions on a rapid march to pursue those who had fled. When these had advanced some distance, and the rear was just visible to those in camp, horsemen came from Quintus Atrius to Caesar to report that in the previous night a very great storm had arisen and that almost all the ships had been damaged and thrown up on shore, because the anchors and cables would not hold, and the sailors and pilots could not cope with the force of the storm;

consequently great damage had resulted from the collision of the ships.

CHAPTER 11

WHEN HE LEARNED OF THIS, Caesar ordered the legions and the cavalry to be recalled, to beat off the enemy on the march, and he himself returned to the ships. He saw with his own eyes almost the same things he had learned from the messengers and the dispatches from Atrius—about forty ships were lost, but the rest, it seemed, could be repaired, though with great trouble. He therefore picked out mechanics from the legions, and ordered others to be summoned from the continent; he wrote to Labienus to build as many ships as possible with the help of the legions he had with him. Although the task involved much labor and effort, Caesar himself decided that it was best that all the ships be beached and joined with the camp by one fortification. On this task he spent about ten days, not allowing the soldiers to interrupt their work even at night. When the ships had been beached and the camp had been well fortified, he left the same forces as before to guard the ships, and set out to the same place from which he had returned. When he had come there, he found that still greater forces of the Britons had assembled there from all sides; the supreme command and management of the war had been entrusted by common consent to Cassivellaunus, whose territory is separated from the maritime states by a river called the Thames, about eighty miles from the sea. Previously continuous wars had taken place between him and the other states; but greatly alarmed by our arrival, the Britons had placed him in command of the whole war.

CHAPTER 12

THE INTERIOR OF BRITAIN is inhabited by those who, according to their own tradition, are said to have originated in the island itself; the seacoast is inhabited by those who crossed over from Belgium for the purpose of plunder and war; nearly all of the latter bear the names of the states from which they sprang before they came to Britain; after the war they remained there and began to cultivate the fields. The population is exceedingly large, their buildings are very numerous, very much like those of the Gauls, and they have a great number of cattle. They use either bronze or gold coins, or, instead of coined money, iron bars weighed to a certain standard. Tin is found in the inland regions, iron in the maritime districts, but of that there is only a small supply. They use imported bronze. As in Gaul, there is timber of every kind, except beech and fir. They do not consider it right to eat hare, chicken, and goose; but they raise them for pastime and amusement. The region has a milder climate than Gaul, the cold being less severe.

CHAPTER 13

THE ISLAND IS TRIANGULAR in shape, and one of its sides lies opposite Gaul. One corner of this side, which is near Kent, where almost all the ships from Gaul put in, faces east, and the lower corner faces south. This side extends about five hundred miles. The second side lies towards Spain and the west; and on this side lies Ireland, a half smaller, as it is thought, than Britain, but reached by a passage just as long as that from Gaul to Britain. Halfway across between Britain and Ireland is an island, called the Isle of Man; moreover, several smaller islands are supposed to lie off the coast on this side; about these islands some have written that, at the winter solstice, night lasts for about thirty whole days. We could discover nothing about this by inquiries, except that by exact measurements made with a water clock, we found that the nights were shorter than on the continent. According to the opinion of the Britons, the length of this side is seven hundred miles. The third side lies towards the north; no land lies opposite it; but a corner of that side faces principally Germany. This side is supposed to be eight hundred miles long. Thus the whole island is two thousand miles in circumference.

CHAPTER 14

OF ALL THE BRITONS by far the most civilized are the inhabitants of Kent, which is wholly a maritime district; their customs differ but little from those of the Gauls. Those living in the interior for the most part do not sow grain, but live on milk and meat, and clothe themselves with skins. All the Britons, indeed dye their bodies with woad, which produces a bluish color, and on this account they are rather wild-looking in battle. They wear their hair long, and shave every part of the body except the head and the upper lip. Groups of ten or twelve men, particularly brothers with brothers and fathers with sons, have wives in common; but the children born of these unions are considered to belong to the man to whose house the mother was conducted as a bride.

CHAPTER 15

THE CAVALRY and charioteers of the enemy fought fiercely with our cavalry on the march, with the result, however, that our men were superior in all respects, and drove them to the woods and hills; after killing many of the enemy, our men pursued too eagerly, and lost some of their own men. But after an interval, when our men were off their guard and engaged in the fortification of the camp, the enemy suddenly rushed out of the woods, and attacking those who were on guard before the camp, fought fiercely. Caesar sent two cohorts, the first of two legions, to help them; when these had taken up their position at a very short distance from each other, as our men were thoroughly frightened by the strange kind of fighting, the enemy most boldly broke through between them and retreated in safety. On that day a tribune of the soldiers, named Quintus Laberius Durus, was killed. The enemy were driven back after more cohorts had been sent against them.

CHAPTER 16

THROUGHOUT THIS ENGAGEMENT, which took place in front of the camp in sight of all, it was evident that since our men, because of their heavy arms, could not pursue the retreating enemy and dared not leave their standards, they were poorly fitted for this kind of enemy. It was also evident that our cavalry fought with great danger, because the Britons generally would fall back purposely, and when they had drawn our men off a little from the legions, would leap down from their chariots and fight on foot with the advantage on their side. There was the further fact that they never fought in close formation, but in small bodies and at great distances, and had reserves stationed in various places, so that they might relieve one another in turn, the vigorous and fresh taking the place of the weary.

CHAPTER 17

THE NEXT DAY the enemy halted on hills at a distance from our camp, and began to appear in small bodies and to attack our cavalry more feebly than the day before. But at noon, when Caesar had sent three legions and the entire cavalry with the lieutenant Gaius Trebonius to get forage, from all directions they suddenly rushed upon the foragers so vehemently that they did not hold back from the standards of the legions. Our men attacked them fiercely and drove them back, and did not stop in their pursuit until the

cavalry, relying on the support of the legions they
saw behind them, drove the enemy in headlong flight;
they slew a great number of them, and gave the rest no
chance to rally, make a stand, or leap from their
chariots. Immediately after this rout, the British auxiliaries that had assembled from all quarters departed,
and after that time the enemy never engaged us at
their full strength.

CHAPTER 18

HAVING LEARNED the enemy's plan,
Caesar led his army into the territory of Cassivellaunus
to the river Thames, which can be crossed on foot in
only one place, and even here with difficulty. When he
had arrived there, he perceived that on the opposite
bank of the river large forces of the enemy had been
drawn up. The bank was protected by sharp stakes
driven in front, and stakes of the same kind fixed under
the water were concealed by the river. When he had
learned these things from prisoners and deserters, Caesar sent the cavalry ahead and ordered the legions to
follow immediately. But though they were in water up
to the chin, the soldiers advanced with such speed and
such spirit that the enemy could not withstand the attack of the legions and of the cavalry, but left the banks
and took to flight.

CHAPTER 19

CASSIVELLAUNUS, as we stated above, giving up all hope of a general engagement, dismissed the greater part of his forces, and with about four thousand charioteers, who stayed behind, watched our line of march; withdrawing a little from the road, he concealed himself in inaccessible and wooded places. In those districts through which he had learned that we intended to march, he drove the cattle and the inhabitants from the fields into the woods; and whenever our cavalry dashed forth into the fields to get plunder and to devastate the country more freely, he sent out charioteers from the woods by all the roads and paths, and, to the great danger of our cavalry, engaged them in battle, and by the fear of this danger kept them from roaming farther afield. The only course left to Caesar was not to allow the cavalry to move too far from the main body of the legions, and to do as much harm to the enemy by laying waste their fields and burning their possessions as the legionary soldiers could accomplish by strenuous marches.

CHAPTER 20

IN THE MEANTIME, the Trinovantes, about the strongest state in those parts, a state from which young Mandubracius, attaching himself to Caesar, had come to him to the continent (his father had held the kingship in the state, and had been killed by Cassivellaunus, but Mandubracius himself had escaped death by flight) sent ambassadors to Caesar and promised to surrender to him and obey his commands; they begged him to protect Mandubracius from violence at the hands of Cassivellaunus, and to send him to their state as its supreme ruler. Caesar demanded from them forty hostages, and grain for his army, and sent Mandubracius to them. They speedily carried out his orders and sent the full number of hostages and the grain.

CHAPTER 21

WHEN THE TRINOVANTES had been protected and kept from all harm at the hands of our soldiers, the Cenimagni, the Segontiaci, the Ancalites, the Bibroci, and the Cassi sent embassies and surrendered to Caesar. From them he learned that not far from that place was the stronghold of Cassivellaunus, protected by woods and marshes, and that he had assembled there a large number of men and cattle. Now the Britons apply the name "stronghold" to a spot in an inaccessible forest when they have fortified it with a rampart and a trench, and there they usually retire to escape from a hostile raid. To this place Caesar set out with the legions; he found it very well fortified by nature and art; nevertheless he hastened to attack it on two sides. After a little while the enemy could not withstand the attack of our soldiers, and rushed out from another side of the stronghold. A great quantity of cattle was found there, and many of the enemy were caught in their flight and put to death.

CHAPTER 22

WHILE THESE OPERATIONS were going on in these districts, Cassivellaunus sent messengers to Kent, which, as we have shown above, is close to the sea. Four kings, Cingetorix, Carvilius, Taximagulus, and Segovax, ruled these districts. He ordered them to collect all their forces and to make a sudden attack on the naval camp. When these forces had come to the camp, our men made a sally and slew many of them; they also captured Lugotorix, a commander of high rank, and led back their own men unharmed. When this battle was reported to Cassivellaunus, as he had sustained so many losses, and as his territory had been laid waste, and chiefly as he was alarmed by the revolt of the states, he sent envoys to Caesar to negotiate a surrender with the help of the Atrebatian Commius. Since Caesar had decided to pass the winter on the continent because sudden disturbances were likely to break out in Gaul, and since little of the summer was left, and he realized that this could easily be wasted, he demanded hostages and determined what tribute Britain should pay each year to the Roman people. He gave strict orders to Cassivellaunus not to do any harm to Mandubracius or the Trinovantes.

CHAPTER 23

WHEN HE HAD RECEIVED the hostages, he led the army back to the sea, and found the ships repaired. When these had been launched, as he had a great number of prisoners, and some ships had been lost in the storm, he decided to convoy his army back in two trips. And it happened that of so large a number of ships, which made so many voyages in this or in the previous year, not a single ship which carried soldiers was lost; but of the ships which were sent back empty to him from the continent, both those which had disembarked soldiers on the first trip and the sixty which Labienus had afterwards caused to be built, very few reached their destination; almost all of them were driven back to land. Caesar waited some time for these in vain; but lest he be prevented from sailing by the season of the year, as the equinox was close at hand, of necessity he packed the soldiers rather closely; a profound calm ensued, and he set sail at the beginning of the second watch; he reached land at daybreak and brought all the ships safely across.

CHAPTER 24

AFTER THE SHIPS WERE BEACHED, a council of the Gauls was held at Samarobriva. As the crops had been scantier in Gaul that year on account of the drought, Caesar was compelled to station his army in winter quarters, adopting a method different from that of previous years, and to distribute the legions among a larger number of states. One of them he assigned to the lieutenant Gaius Fabius, to be led into the country of the Mirini; a second to Quintus Cicero to be led into the country of the Nervii; a third to Lucius Roscius, to be led into the country of the Esuvii; a fourth he ordered to winter with Titus Labienus among the Remi near the frontier of the Treveri. Three he stationed in Belgium; he placed in command of these the quaestor Marcus Crassus and the lieutenants Lucius Munatius Plancus and Gaius Trebonius. One legion which he had recently enrolled north of the Po and five cohorts he sent into the country of the Eburones, the main part of which lies between the Meuse and the Rhine; these were governed by Ambiorix and Catuvolcus. He ordered the lieutenants Quintus Titurius Sabinus and Lucius Aurunculeius Cotta to assume command of these soldiers. By distributing the legions this way, he thought that he could very easily remedy the shortage of the grain supply. And yet the winter quarters of all these legions, except for the one which he had assigned to Lucius Roscius to be led to the most peaceful and tranquil district, were only one hundred miles apart. He himself in the meantime decided to stay in Gaul until he learned that the legions had reached their destinations and the winter quarters had been fortified.

CHAPTER 25

IN THE COUNTRY of the Carnutes was a man of noble birth, named Tasgetius, whose ancestors had held the sovereignty in their state. In recognition of his efficiency and his loyalty Caesar had restored to

him the position of his ancestors, because in all the
wars he had made use of his extraordinary assistance.
His personal enemies, with the open approval of many
persons of his own state, assassinated him during the
third year of his reign. This crime was reported to
Caesar. Since a large number were implicated, Caesar
feared that the state might revolt at their instigation.
He therefore ordered Lucius Plancus to proceed
quickly with his legion from Belgium to the country of
the Carnutes, to winter there, and to take into custody
and to send to him those whom he found responsible
for the murder of Tasgetius. Meanwhile he was informed by all the lieutenants and the quaestor to whom
he had assigned the legions that they had reached the
winter quarters and that their stations had been fortified.

CHAPTER 26

ABOUT A FORTNIGHT after the Roman
forces had come into winter quarters, a sudden out-
break and revolt was started by Ambiorix and
Catuvolcus; these had met Sabinus and Cotta at the
frontier of their kingdom and brought grain to our
winter quarters, but, induced by a message from the
Treveran Indutiomarus, they stirred up their people,
suddenly fell upon the soldiers who were engaged in
getting wood, and came with a large force to attack the
camp. When our men had speedily taken up arms, had
mounted the rampart, and, sending out Spanish horsemen on one side, had proved victorious in a cavalry
engagement, the enemy, despairing of success, with-

drew their men from the assault. Then, according to their custom, they called loudly for some one of our men to come to a conference. They asserted that there were certain matters which they wished to discuss respecting our mutual interest, whereby they hoped the questions at issue could be settled.

CHAPTER 27

GAIUS ARPINEIUS, a Roman knight, an intimate friend of Quintus Titurius, and Quintus Junius, a Spaniard, who on previous occasions had been frequently sent by Caesar to Ambiorix, were sent to confer with them. To them Ambiorix spoke as follows: He admitted that for Caesar's favors towards him he was very much indebted to him; it was by Caesar's aid that he had been relieved of the tribute which he had been accustomed to pay to his neighbors the Atuatuci, and it was by Caesar's aid that his own son and his brother's son, who had been sent to the Atuatuci as hostages and had been kept among them in slavery and chains, had been restored to him. He had attacked the Roman camp against his own judgment and will; he had been forced by his state to do so; the conditions of his authority were such that the people had as much power over him as he had over the people. Moreover, the state's reason for making war was its inability to resist the sudden conspiracy of the Gauls. He could easily prove that by the insignificance of his own power; for he was not so ignorant as to presume that the Roman people could be conquered by his own unaided forces. This was the common plan of

Gaul; this was the day appointed for attacking all the winter quarters of Caesar, so that no legion might be able to come to the relief of another. Gauls could not easily refuse help to Gauls, especially when it was evident that a plan had been formed for the recovery of their common freedom. Since he had done his duty by them and by his country, he now took account of his obligation to Caesar for his kindnesses. He warned and he begged Titurius, by reason of their old friendship, to have regard for his own safety and that of his soldiers. A large force of German mercenaries had crossed the Rhine; it would arrive in two days. It was for the Romans to decide whether they should lead their forces out of winter quarters before their neighbors could become aware of their intention, and to take them either to Cicero or to Labienus, one of whom was about fifty miles from them, the other a little farther. He promised and confirmed by an oath that he would give them a safe passage through his territory. In doing this, he was looking out for the interest of his own state, because it would be relieved of the burden of the winter quarters, and he was making a return to Caesar for his services. Having delivered this speech, Ambiorix withdrew.

CHAPTER 28

ARPINEIUS AND JUNIUS reported to the lieutenants what they had heard. Greatly disturbed by the unexpected report, although the proposal was made by an enemy, still they thought that it must not be disregarded. They were especially disturbed by this one thing; it was hardly credible that the obscure and insignificant state of the Eburones of its own accord had dared to make war upon the Roman people. Therefore they referred the matter to a council of war, and a great dispute arose among them. Lucius Aurunculeius and several tribunes of the soldiers and the centurions of the first rank thought that nothing should be done rashly, and that they should not leave the winter quarters without Caesar's order. They pointed out that any force of Gauls, even great forces of Germans, could be resisted in fortified winter quarters; they had proof of it in the fact that they had most valiantly withstood the first attack of the enemy, even inflicting many wounds upon them; there was no difficulty about supplies; in the meantime reinforcements would come both from the nearest winter quarters and from Caesar; finally, what was more undignified or more disgraceful than to decide supreme issues on the advice of an enemy?

CHAPTER 29

IN REPLY TO THIS, Titurius kept protesting loudly that it would be too late to act when larger forces of the enemy, joined with the Germans, had assembled, or when some disaster had been suffered in the neighboring winter quarters. There was little time for deliberation. He believed that Caesar had gone to Italy; otherwise the Carnutes would not have planned the murder of Tasgetius; and if Caesar were near, the Eburones would not have come to our camp with such great contempt for us. He had regard not for the enemy as adviser, but for the facts of the case. The Rhine was near; the death of Ariovistus and our previous victories were a cause of great vexation to the Germans, Gaul was ablaze with wrath at so many insults heaped upon her since she had been brought under the authority of the Roman people, and at the eclipse of her former military glory. Finally, who could persuade himself that Ambiorix would have resorted to a plan of that kind unless he had been sure of success? His own view was safe in either case: If nothing serious should happen, they would reach the nearest legion without any danger; but if all Gaul were to conspire with the Germans, their only safety lay in speedy action. Where would the plan of Cotta and of those who disagreed with Titurius lead? There might be no immediate danger in it, but there was certainly famine to fear from a protracted seige.

CHAPTER 30

AFTER THIS DISCUSSION on both sides, when vigorous opposition was still offered by Cotta and the leading centurions, Sabinus, raising his voice so that a large part of the soldiers could hear him, exclaimed: "Have your own way, if you will. I am not the one to be most alarmed by the danger of death. But the soldiers will understand; if any disaster occurs, they will hold you responsible; if you would consent, these would be united on the day after tomorrow with the nearest winter quarters and would face the war in common with the rest, and would not perish by the sword or by famine, abandoned and treated as outlaws."

CHAPTER 31

ALL ROSE from the council table, seized the two leaders by the hand, and begged them not to endanger the issue by their disagreement and obstinacy; there was no real difficulty, whether they stayed or departed, if only all felt the same way and approved one plan; but they saw no safety in disagreement. The debate continued till midnight. At last Cotta, greatly distressed, was induced to yield, and the opinion of Sabinus prevailed. It was announced that they would set out at dawn. The rest of the night was spent without sleep, since each soldier was looking over his possessions to see what he could take with him, and what part of his winter equipment he would be forced to leave behind. They thought of every reason why they could not remain without danger, and why the danger would be increased by the exhaustion of the soldiers and their loss of sleep. At dawn they left the camp like men convinced that they had been given advice not by an enemy, but by a very friendly person; they therefore marched in a very long line, encumbered with very heavy baggage.

CHAPTER 32

WHEN THE ENEMY INFERRED from the noise during the night and the failure on the part of the Romans to retire for the night that they intended to depart, they posted an ambush at two points in the woods, in a suitable and secret place about two miles

off, and there they awaited the arrival of the Romans.
When the greater part of the Roman column had descended into a large defile, they suddenly made their
appearance on either side of that defile and began to
harass the rear, to prevent the van from climbing up
the hill, and to join battle on ground most unfavorable
to our men.

CHAPTER 33

ONLY THEN DID TITURIUS, who had
foreseen no such thing, become greatly alarmed; he
rushed from place to place and tried to arrange his
cohorts; yet even this he did faint-heartedly and in such
a way that all his resources seemed to fail him; this
generally happens to those who are compelled to form
a plan on the spur of the moment. But Cotta, who had
thought that this might happen on the march and for
that reason had not been in favor of leaving the
camp, did everything possible to provide for the common safety; in addressing and encouraging the soldiers
he discharged the duties of a general, in battle those of
a soldier. Since on account of the length of the column
Cotta and Sabinus could not easily look after everything in person and provide for the necessary action in
each place, they gave orders that the word be passed to
abandon the baggage and to form a circle. This measure, which is not to be criticized in such an emergency,
had an unfortunate result; for it diminished the hope of
our soldiers, and made the enemy more eager for the
fight, since the Roman action seemed to be prompted
by the greatest fear and despair. Moreover it hap-

pened, as was inevitable, that the soldiers on all sides were leaving their standards, and each of them hastened to seek and carry off from the baggage whatever he thought most dear; everywhere there was shouting and weeping.

CHAPTER 34

THE ENEMY, on the other hand, maintained their presence of mind. Their leaders ordered the command to be given along the line that no man should leave his post: the booty was theirs, and whatever the Romans left was reserved for them; therefore, they must realize that everything depended on victory. Our men, though deserted by their leader and by fortune, still placed all hope of safety in valor, and as often as a cohort dashed forward, a great number of the enemy would fall on that side. When Ambiorix saw this, he ordered the command to be given that his soldiers hurl their missiles from afar and not come too close to the Romans, and in whatever direction the Romans made an attack, they give way there (saying that because of their light arms and their daily training no harm would be done to them), but that they pursue the Romans when they were returning to their standards.

CHAPTER 35

THIS ORDER WAS MOST carefully obeyed. Whenever a cohort left the circle and made an attack, the enemy would flee very swiftly. In the meantime, that part of the circle was unavoidably exposed, and

missiles fell on its unprotected flank. And when the
soldiers began to return to the place from which they
had started, they were surrounded both by those who
had given way and by those who had remained in
their positions; but if the Romans wished to keep their
place in the circle, there was no opportunity left for
valor, and, being so closely packed, they could not escape the missiles hurled by so many men. Nevertheless,
although they were harassed by so many difficulties and
had received many wounds, they still offered resistance;
a great part of the day had gone by while the battle
lasted from daybreak till the eighth hour, yet our men
did nothing unworthy of them. Then Titus Balventius,
a brave man of great influence, who the year before
had been chief centurion, had both his thighs pierced
by a javelin; Quintus Lucanius, an officer of the same
rank, was killed while fighting most bravely when he
came to the rescue of his son, who had been surrounded; the lieutenant Lucius Cotta, while encouraging all the cohorts and centuries, was struck full in the
face by a slingshot.

CHAPTER 36

WHEN QUINTUS TITURIUS, alarmed by
these events, had caught sight of Ambiorix at a distance addressing his men, he sent to him his interpreter, Gnaeus Pompey, to ask him to spare him and
his soldiers. Thus appealed to, Ambiorix replied that if
he wished to confer with him, he had his permission to
do so; as far as the safety of the soldiers was concerned, he hoped that that request might be granted

by the army; to Titurius himself certainly no harm
would be done, and to that he pledged his word.
Titurius consulted with the wounded Cotta whether it
appeared right for them to withdraw from the battle
and together confer with Ambiorix; he hoped that he
would obtain his request that they and the soldiers
might be spared. Cotta refused to go to an armed
enemy, and persisted in that refusal.

CHAPTER 37

SABINUS ORDERED the tribunes of the
soldiers, whom he had with him at the time, and
the centurions of the first rank to follow him, and when
he had come quite near to Ambiorix and was ordered to lay down his arms, he obeyed, and commanded his men to do the same. While they were dis-
cussing terms, and Ambiorix purposely was making
too long a speech, Sabinus was gradually surrounded
and killed. Then, according to their custom, they
shouted, "Victory," and with a loud yell attacked our
men and threw the ranks into confusion. There Lucius
Cotta was killed fighting, together with the greatest
part of the soldiers. The rest retreated to the camp
from which they had marched out. One of them, the
eaglebearer Lucius Petrosidius, although he was hard
pressed by a great number of the enemy, threw the
eagle within the rampart and was himself killed while
fighting most bravely before the camp. The rest with
difficulty kept off the attack till nightfall; in the night,
despairing of safety, they killed one another to a
man. A few who had escaped from the battle made

their way by hazardous paths through the woods to the winter quarters of the lieutenant Titus Labienus, and informed him of what had happened.

CHAPTER 38

ELATED BY THIS VICTORY, Ambiorix at once marched with his cavalry into the territory of the Atuatuci, which was close to his kingdom; he stopped his march neither by day nor by night, and ordered his infantry to follow him closely. He stirred up the Atuatuci by the report of what had been done. The next day he came into the territory of the Nervii, and urged them not to lose the chance of freeing themselves forever and of taking vengeance on the Romans for the wrongs they had suffered; two lieutenants, he told them, had been slain, and a large part of the army had perished; it would be easy to fall suddenly upon the legion which was wintering under the command of Cicero and destroy it; he promised his cooperation in that enterprise. By this speech he easily won over the Nervii.

CHAPTER 39

ACCORDINGLY MESSENGERS were at once dispatched to the Ceutrones, the Grudii, the Levaci, the Pleumoxii, and the Geidumni, all of whom were under the control of the Nervii; they raised forces as large as possible, and rushed suddenly upon the winter quarters of Cicero, who had not yet received the news of the death of Titurius. In his case also it happened, as was inevitable, that some soldiers who had gone off into the woods to get timber for the fortification of the camp were cut off by the sudden arrival of the enemy's cavalry. After these had been surrounded, the Eburones, the Nervii, the Atuatuci, and the allies and dependents of all of them began the attack on the legion. Our men quickly took up arms and mounted the rampart. They held out with difficulty that day, since the enemy placed all their hope in speed, and were confident that if they won this victory, they would be victorious ever after.

CHAPTER 40

A DISPATCH was immediately sent to Caesar by Cicero; he promised large rewards to the messengers if they delivered it safe; but as all the roads were blocked, the messengers were intercepted. During the night fully one hundred and twenty towers were erected out of the timber which the soldiers had collected for the fortification of the camp; with incredible speed the defects in the fortification were made good. The following day, the enemy, having assembled still greater forces, attacked the camp and filled up the trench. Our men resisted in the same manner as on the day before. The same thing happened on successive days. Our soldiers worked incessantly through the night; no chance to rest was given to the sick or wounded. Whatever was needed to meet the next day's assault was prepared during the night; many stakes with points hardened in the fire and a large number of

wall-pikes were made ready; the towers were provided
with floors, battlements, and breastworks of wattle
were attached to the towers. Cicero himself, though he
was in very poor health, gave himself no rest even at
night, so that he was actually forced to spare himself
by the pressure and entreaties of the soldiers.

CHAPTER 41

THEN THE LEADERS AND CHIEFS of the
Nervii, who had a pretext for an interview and a reason for being well-disposed towards Cicero, said that
they desired to confer with him. When their request
was granted, they used the same arguments which
Ambiorix had used with Titurius: All Gaul was in
arms; the Germans had crossed the Rhine; and the winter quarters of Caesar and of the others were being
attacked. They also reported the death of Sabinus;
they pointed to Ambiorix in order to inspire credence.
Cicero and his men, they said, were deluding themselves if they hoped for any help at all from those
who were themselves in desperate straits. Nevertheless,
they had this feeling towards Cicero and the Roman
people that they refused nothing except winter quarters, as they did not want this custom to become an
established practice; so far as the Gauls were concerned, they might depart in safety from their winter
quarters and proceed without fear in whatever direction they pleased. To this Cicero made but one reply:
it was not the practice of the Roman people to accept
terms from an enemy in arms: if they wished to lay
down their arms and send an embassy to Caesar, they

might employ him as mediator; he hoped that in view of Caesar's sense of justice they would receive what they asked.

CHAPTER 42

FOILED IN THIS HOPE of deceiving Cicero, the Nervii surrounded the winter quarters with a rampart ten feet high and a trench fifteen feet wide. This they had learned from us by observing our practice in previous years, and having taken some prisoners from our army, they were instructed by them. But as they had no stock of iron tools suitable for this purpose, they were forced to cut the sods with their swords, and to take out the earth with their bare hands and in their cloaks. From this circumstance one can infer the large number of their men; for in less than three hours they completed a fortification three miles in circumference. During the following days, under the direction of the same prisoners, they began to prepare and construct towers in proportion to the height of the rampart, also grappling hooks and movable sheds.

CHAPTER 43

ON THE SEVENTH DAY of the siege, a very strong wind sprang up, and the Gauls began to sling red-hot balls made of softened clay and to hurl heated javelins at the huts, which, in Gallic fashion, had been covered with thatch. The huts quickly caught fire, and because of the force of the wind, the fire spread to every corner of the camp. With a loud shout, as if victory were already won and assured, the enemy began to move up their towers and movable sheds and to mount the rampart with scaling ladders. But so great was the courage of our soldiers and such their presence of mind that, though they were being scorched on all sides by the flames and harassed by a very large number of missiles and though they realized that all their baggage and all their possessions were on fire, not only did no one leave the rampart in order to withdraw, but hardly anyone even looked around, and then all of them fought with the greatest vigor and courage. This day was by far the most serious for our men; but the result was that on that day the largest number of the enemy was wounded and slain, for they were crowded together close up to the rampart, and those in the back would not give those in front a chance to draw back. When the flames had abated a little, and one of the enemy's towers was moved up in one place and was touching the rampart, the centurions of the third cohort drew back from the place where they were standing and moved back all their men; they then began to invite the enemy by signs and shouts to come inside if they wished; but not one of them dared to advance. They were then forced back by volleys of stones from every side, and their tower was set on fire.

CHAPTER 44

THERE WERE IN THAT LEGION two very brave centurions, who were nearing the first rank, Titus Pullo and Lucius Vorenus. These were continually arguing with each other which should have the preference over the other, and every year they contended for advancement with the keenest rivalry. Of these Pullo, when the fighting was the very fiercest before the fortifications, shouted: "Why do you hesitate, Vorenus? What better opportunity of proving your valor are you waiting for? This day shall decide our quarrels." Having said this, he advanced outside the fortifications and rushed upon the part of the enemy which appeared the thickest. Vorenus did not remain within the rampart; fearing the adverse opinion of his fellow soldiers, he followed close after. Then, at a moderate distance, Pullo threw his javelin at the enemy and transfixed one of the crowd as he ran forward. When this man was struck down unconscious, the enemy protected him with their shields, and all of them threw their spears at Pullo, and gave him no chance of advancing farther. Pullo's shield was pierced, and the dart lodged in his sword belt. This mishap turned his scabbard aside, and impeded his right hand as he was attempting to draw his sword; and while he was thus hampered, he was surrounded by the enemy. His rival Vorenus ran to his rescue and helped him in his difficulty. At once the whole crowd turned from Pullo on him; they thought that Pullo had been killed by the dart. Vorenus engaged in close fighting with the sword, and having slain one man, forced

back the rest a little; while he pressed on too eagerly,
stumbling into a hollow, he fell down. As he in his
turn was surrounded, Pullo brought him help. After
killing several men, both men returned unharmed to
camp covered with the greatest glory. Thus Fortune
shifted the positions of both in rivalry and combat so
that each rival helped and saved the other, and so that
it could not be determined which of the two should
seem worthy to be considered superior to the other in
point of valor.

CHAPTER 45

THE HARDER AND MORE VIOLENT the
siege became day-by-day (chiefly because a great number of the soldiers were incapacitated by wounds, and
the burden had fallen on a small number of defenders), the more frequently dispatches and messengers
were sent to Caesar. Some of these messengers were
caught and tortured to death in sight of our soldiers.
There was in the camp one Nervian named Vertico, a
man of good family, who at the beginning of the siege
had fled to Cicero for refuge, and had sworn an oath of
fidelity to him. By the hope of freedom and by great
rewards this man persuaded a slave of his to carry a
dispatch to Caesar. This dispatch the slave carried
forth tied to a javelin, and, as he was himself a Gaul,
he mingled with Gauls without arousing any suspicion, and reached Caesar. From him Caesar learned
about the danger of Cicero and his legion.

CHAPTER 46

CAESAR RECEIVED the dispatch about the eleventh hour of the day, and immediately sent a messenger to the quaestor Marcus Crassus, whose winter quarters were twenty-five miles distant from him in the country of the Bellovaci; he ordered the legion to set out at midnight and come to him with all speed. Crassus set out with the messenger. Another messenger was sent to the lieutenant Gaius Fabius, directing him to lead his legion into the territory of the Atrebates, through which he knew he would have to march. He wrote to Labienus to come with his legion to the frontier of the Nervii, if he could do so without risk. Caesar did not think that he ought to wait for the rest of the army, because it was a little too far away; he assembled about four hundred horsemen from the nearest winter quarters.

CHAPTER 47

ABOUT THE THIRD HOUR he was informed by the advance guards of Crassus of his arrival, and on that day Caesar advanced twenty miles. He put Crassus in charge of Samarobriva and assigned him a legion, because he was leaving there the baggage of the army, the hostages of the states, the state documents, and all the grain which he had collected there to last through the winter. Fabius, as he had been ordered, with very little delay met him on the march with his legion. Labienus had learned of the death of Sabinus and the destruction of his cohorts; as all the forces of the Treveri had come against him, he feared that, if he made a departure from his winter quarters as if in flight, he would be unable to withstand the attack of the enemy, especially since he knew that they were elated by their recent victory. Accordingly, he sent back a dispatch to Caesar, explaining how dangerous it would be for him to lead his legion out of winter quarters. He wrote a full account of what had taken place in the country of the Eburones, and he informed him that all the cavalry and infantry of the Treveri had encamped three miles from his own camp.

CHAPTER 48

CAESAR APPROVED Labienus' decision. Although he had been disappointed in his expectation of having three legions and had been reduced to two, he thought that speed was the only possible way to secure the safety of all. By forced marches he came to the territory of the Nervii. There he learned from prisoners what was going on in Cicero's camp, and in how great danger his position was. Then with great rewards he prevailed upon one of the Gallic horsemen to deliver a letter to Cicero. This he sent written in Greek characters, so that, if the letter were intercepted, the enemy might not find out our plans. He directed the messenger, if he could not reach the camp, to throw his spear, with the letter fastened to the thong, inside the fortifications of the camp. In the letter he wrote that he had set out with the legions and would

be there shortly; he urged him to keep up his old courage. Fearing danger, the Gaul threw the spear, as he
had been instructed. This accidentally stuck in a
tower, and was not noticed by our men for two days;
on the third day it was seen by a soldier, taken down,
and brought to Cicero. After he had read it through,
he read it aloud to an assembly of the soldiers, and
filled all with the greatest joy. Then the smoke of
burning villages was seen in the distance, and this removed all doubt of the coming of the legions.

CHAPTER 49

THE GAULS, having been informed by
their scouts of Caesar's approach, raised the siege and
directed their march towards Caesar with all their
forces. These numbered about sixty thousand armed
men. When the opportunity presented itself, Cicero
again asked the same Vertico, whom we mentioned
above, for a Gaul to carry a letter to Caesar. In this
letter he warned Caesar to proceed cautiously and
carefully; he reported that the enemy had withdrawn
from him and had directed the entire force against him.
When this letter was brought to Caesar about midnight, he informed his soldiers of its contents, and encouraged them for the fight. The next day, at dawn,
he broke camp, and, after advancing about four miles,
he caught sight of the enemy's forces across a brook
flowing in a wide valley. It was extremely hazardous
for such small Roman forces to fight on unfavorable
ground; but as he knew that Cicero had been freed
from blockade, he thought that he could slacken his

pace without anxiety. He halted, and fortified his camp on as favorable a site as possible. Although this camp was small in itself, as it contained barely seven thousand men and no baggage, nevertheless he made it still smaller by making the passages as narrow as possible, with the object of incurring the utmost contempt on the part of the enemy. Meanwhile he sent scouts in all directions to find out by what route he could most conveniently cross the valley.

CHAPTER 50

ON THAT DAY slight cavalry skirmishes took place near the brook, but both armies maintained their positions: the Gauls, because they were waiting for larger forces which had not yet arrived; Caesar, on the other hand, to see if by pretending fear, he could entice the enemy to a position favorable to himself, so that he might fight on his side of the valley, in front of the camp; or, if unsuccessful in that, to cross the valley and the brook with less danger after reconnoitering the routes. At dawn the cavalry of the enemy approached the camp and joined battle with our cavalry. Caesar purposely ordered the cavalry to give way and to retreat to the camp; at the same time he ordered the camp to be fortified with a higher rampart on all sides, the gates to be barricaded, and in the execution of these orders the men should rush about as much as possible and act with a pretense of fear.

CHAPTER 51

ENTICED BY ALL THESE proceedings, the enemy led their forces across, and drew up their line on unfavorable ground; and as our men had been withdrawn even from the rampart, they approached nearer and hurled their missiles from all sides into the fortification; they sent heralds around with orders to announce that if anyone, Gaul or Roman, would go over to them before the third hour, he might do so without any danger; after that time there would be no chance to do so. They showed such contempt for our men that, as the gates had been barricaded for show with single rows of sods, and the enemy thought that they could not break in that way, some began to pull down the rampart with their bare hands, others to fill up the trenches. Then Caesar made a sally from all the gates, and sending out the cavalry, he quickly routed the enemy so thoroughly that not one man stood his ground to fight. He killed a great number of them and stripped all of their arms.

CHAPTER 52

CAESAR WAS AFRAID to pursue them too far, because woods and marshes were in the way and because he saw that no opportunity was left for inflicting even a trifling loss upon them; and so, with all his forces intact, he reached Cicero the same day. He marvelled at the built towers, the sheds, and the fortifications of the enemy. When the legion was drawn up for review, he found that not one soldier in ten had escaped unwounded; from all this he judged with what danger and with what courage the operations had been handled. He warmly praised Cicero for his heroic service, and also the legion; he addressed individually the centurions and the tribunes of the soldiers, whose valor, as Cicero assured him, had been exceptional. From the prisoners he received more definite information about the disaster of Sabinus and Cotta. The following day he assembled the soldiers, set forth what had happened, consoled and encouraged the men; he also told them that the loss which had been incurred through the culpable rashness of a lieutenant should be borne with the greater tranquillity, since by the favor of the immortal gods and their own valor the disaster had been atoned for, leaving to the enemy no lasting joy, and to them not too long a grief.

CHAPTER 53

MEANWHILE THE REPORT of Caesar's victory was brought to Labienus by the Remi with such incredible speed that, although Labienus was about sixty miles away from Cicero's winter quarters, and Caesar had not arrived there until after the ninth hour, before midnight a shout arose at the gates of the camp, announcing the victory and offering the congratulations of the Remi to Labienus. When this report was brought to the Treveri, Indutiomarus, who had decided to attack the camp of Labienus the following day, fled by night, and withdrew all his forces into the country of the Treveri. Caesar sent Fabius with his legion back

to his winter quarters; he himself decided to winter
with three legions in three separate camps near Samarobriva, and, because great disturbances had arisen in
Gaul, he determined to stay with the army himself during the whole winter. For when the report of the death
of Sabinus reached the Gauls, almost all the states of
Gaul were deliberating about war, sending messengers
and embassies in all directions, inquiring what plans
the other tribes were making, and where the war
should start, and holding meetings at night in secluded
places. No part of the whole winter passed without anxiety for Caesar; he was continually receiving some information concerning the plans and uprising of the
Gauls. Among other reports he was informed by Lucius Roscius, whom he had put in command of the
Thirteenth Legion, that large forces of Gauls from
those states which were called Aremorican had assembled to attack him and had encamped not more than
eight miles away from his winter quarters, but, when
they had received word of Caesar's victory, had departed so swiftly that their departure seemed like a
flight.

CHAPTER 54

CAESAR SUMMONED to his camp the
leading men of each state; by frightening some with
the assurance that he knew what was going on and by
encouraging others, he kept a great part of Gaul in allegiance. The Senones, however, an especially powerful and influential state among the Gauls, attempted,
with the decision of the state, to put to death Cavarinus,
whom Caesar had appointed king among them; his

brother Moritasgus had held the sovereignty at the time of Caesar's arrival in Gaul, and his ancestors had also held the sovereignty before. When Cavarinus got wind of their plot and fled, they pursued him up to the frontier and drove him from his kingdom and home. They then sent envoys to Caesar to apologize for their action, but when he ordered their senate to come to him in a body, they did not obey his command. The fact that some men had been found to become the leaders in a war against us made so deep an impression on the natives and produced such a change of feeling in all of them that there was scarcely a state that was not suspected by us. The only exceptions were the Aedui and the Remi, whom Caesar always held in special esteem, the Aedui for their long-standing and unbroken loyalty towards the Roman people, the Remi for their recent services in the Gallic war. And this is perhaps not altogether surprising for many reasons, especially because those who previously surpassed all nations in military courage resented the fact that they had lost so much of that reputation that they had to submit to the rule of the Roman people.

CHAPTER 55

THE TREVERI AND INDUTIOMARUS allowed no part of the entire winter to pass without sending embassies across the Rhine, tampering with the states, promising them money, and asserting that, as a large part of our army had been killed, a much smaller part was left. But no German state could be induced to cross the river; they had tried it twice, they said, in the war under Ariovistus and at the time of the migration of the Tencteri; they would not tempt fortune further. Though disappointed in this hope, Indutiomarus none the less began to raise troops, to train them, to procure horses from his neighbors, and to win over to his side by large rewards exiles and criminals from all over Gaul. By these means he had already secured for himself such great influence in Gaul that embassies flocked to him from all directions, seeking his favor and friendship for their states and for themselves.

CHAPTER 56

WHEN INDUTIOMARUS SAW that people were coming to him of their own accord, that on the one hand the Senones and the Carnutes were spurred on by their guilty consciences and that on the other hand the Nervii and the Atuatuci were preparing for war against the Romans, and that he would not lack forces of volunteers if he began to advance from his own territory, he proclaimed an armed convention. This procedure, according to the practice of the Gauls, constitutes the beginning of a war; by a law common to all, all male adults generally attend it in arms; whoever comes last is put to death with every kind of torture in sight of the assembly. At this convention Indutiomarus declared Cingetorix, the leader of the rival faction, his own son-in-law, an enemy and confiscated his property. Cingetorix, as we mentioned above, had attached himself to Caesar and remained loyal to him. After completing this business, Indutiomarus next informed the assembly that he had been summoned by the Senones and the Carnutes, and several other states of Gaul, and that he intended to march to them through the territory of the Remi, laying waste their country, but before doing that to attack the camp of Labienus. He then instructed them what he wanted done.

CHAPTER 57

SINCE LABIENUS REMAINED in a camp very strongly protected by the nature of the ground and by fortifications, he felt no anxiety for himself and the legion, but he thought that he ought not let slip the chance of fighting a successful battle. Accordingly, when he had learned from Cingetorix and his relatives about the speech which Indutiomarus had delivered in the convention, he sent messengers to the neighboring states and summoned cavalry from all quarters; he set a certain day for them to assemble. In the meantime, almost every day Indutiomarus with all his cavalry would roam close to the Roman camp, now to acquaint himself with its situation, now to exchange some words with our soldiers or to intimidate them, and usually all the horsemen would throw javelins over the rampart. Labienus kept his men within the fortification, and tried by all possible means to give the enemy the impression that he was afraid.

CHAPTER 58

INDUTIOMARUS WAS daily coming up to the Roman camp, showing more and more contempt for the enemy; in a single night Labienus brought into the camp the cavalry of all the neighboring states, which he had caused to be summoned, and by setting a guard he kept all his men within camp so carefully that this fact could by no means be reported or carried to the Treveri. Meanwhile, according to his daily practice, Indutiomarus came up to the camp, and spent a great part of the day there; his cavalry hurled javelins, and with insulting language called our men out to fight. No reply was given by our men; towards evening, when they thought it best, the enemy began to depart in scattered groups. Suddenly Labienus sent out all the cavalry from two gates; he gave the strictest orders that, after they had frightened the enemy and put them to flight (which he foresaw would happen, as it actually did), they should all go after Indutiomarus alone, and no one was to wound any man until he saw the commander of the enemy slain. For Labienus did not wish that the delay caused by the pursuit of the rest should give Indutiomarus time to escape. He offered great rewards to those who should kill him, and sent up some cohorts to assist the cavalry. Fortune favored the general's plan; since all were making for him alone, they caught Indutiomarus in the very act of fording a river, slew him, and brought his head back to camp. As they were returning, the cavalry pursued and killed all they could. Learning of this, all the forces of the Eburones and the Nervii which had assembled departed, and after this achievement Caesar found Gaul somewhat more tranquil.

BOOK VI

CHAPTER 1

FOR MANY REASONS Caesar expected a greater revolt in Gaul; he therefore decided to levy fresh troops with the help of his lieutenants Marcus Silanus, Gaius Antistius Reginus, and Titus Sextius. At the same time he asked Gnaeus Pompey, now proconsul, who while still retaining his military command was staying near Rome for political reasons, to order those men whom he as consul had enlisted in Cisalpine Gaul to join the colors and to proceed to Caesar; he thought it was of great importance, not only for the present but also for the future, that Gaul should be of the opinion that the resources of Italy were great enough not only to repair in a short time any loss sustained in war, but even to increase the size of our forces. When Pompey had granted this request for the public good and out of friendship, Caesar quickly completed the levy with the aid of his officers, and before the end of the winter three legions were formed and brought to him. Thus he doubled the number of the cohorts lost with Quintus Titurius, and by his speed and strengthened forces he showed the Gauls what the organization and resources of the Roman people could accomplish.

CHAPTER 2

AFTER INDUTIOMARUS had been slain, as we have shown, the chief command was conferred by the Treveri upon his relatives. They did not stop tampering with the neighboring Germans and promising them money. As they could not prevail upon their neighbors to join them, they tried those farther off. Having won over some states, they strengthened the compact with one another by an oath, and hostages were given as a guarantee for the payment of the promised money. They associated Ambiorix with themselves by an alliance and treaty. Caesar found this out, and saw preparations for war going on everywhere. The Nervii, the Atuatuci, the Menapii, together with all the Germans on this side of the Rhine, were under arms; the Senones did not come at his command, but were conspiring with the Carnutes and the neighboring states; the Germans were being tampered with by frequent embassies of the Treveri. Caesar therefore thought that he ought to prepare for war earlier than usual.

CHAPTER 3

ACCORDINGLY, BEFORE THE END of the winter, he assembled the four nearest legions and marched suddenly into the territory of the Nervii. Before they could either assemble or escape, he captured a large number of cattle and men and gave them as booty to his soldiers. He laid waste their fields, forced the Nervii to surrender and to give him hostages. Having speedily finished this undertaking, he led his legions back into winter quarters. At the beginning of spring he called a council of Gaul, according to his practice, and all came except the Senones, the Carnutes, and the Treveri. Caesar therefore considered this the beginning of an armed rebellion, and, that it might be clear that he considered this more important than anything else, he transferred the assembly to Lutetia, a town of the Parisii. These were neighbors of the Senones, and within the memory of their fathers had united with them to form one state, but were thought to have had no share in the present plot. Having announced his decision from the platform, on the same day he set out with his legions against the Senones, and arrived there by forced marches.

CHAPTER 4

ON LEARNING of Caesar's coming, Acco, who had been the leader of this conspiracy, ordered the population to assemble in their strongholds. They were trying to do so; but before they could accomplish their object, word was brought to them that the Romans were at hand. Of necessity they gave up the plan, and sent envoys to Caesar to beg for pardon. They approached him with the support of the Aedui, the protectors of their state from ancient times. At the request of the Aedui Caesar willingly pardoned them and accepted their excuses, because he thought that the summer ought to be devoted to the impending war, not to an investigation. He demanded a hundred hostages

and handed them over to the custody of the Aedui.
Through the intercession of the Remi, whose dependents they were, the Carnutes likewise sent envoys and
hostages to his camp; they received the same replies.
Caesar then brought the business of the council to an
end, and levied cavalry on the states.

CHAPTER 5

THIS PART OF GAUL was now pacified,
and he applied himself with all his heart and soul to the
war against the Treveri and Ambiorix. He ordered Cavarinus to accompany him with the cavalry of the Senones, so that no disturbance might arise in the state
either because of his hot temper or their hatred of him,
which he fully deserved. Having made these arrangements, since he regarded it as certain that Ambiorix
would not engage in battle, he began to consider what
other plans he might have. There were the Menapii,
close to the territory of the Eburones, protected by continuous marshes and forests; they alone in Gaul had
never sent envoys to Caesar to sue for peace. Caesar
knew that ties of friendship existed between them and
Ambiorix; he had also discovered that through the Treveri Ambiorix had established friendly relations with
the Germans. He therefore thought that these supports
should be withdrawn from Ambiorix before he provoked him to war, lest, despairing of safety, he hide
among the Menapii, or be forced to unite with the Germans beyond the Rhine. Having adopted this plan,
Caesar sent the baggage of the whole army to Labienus in the territory of the Treveri, and ordered two

legions to set out to him; he himself proceeded against the Menapii with five lightly equipped legions. The Menapii had raised no army, as they relied on the protection of their position; they fled into the forests and marshes, and gathered all their possessions there.

CHAPTER 6

CAESAR DIVIDED his forces with the lieutenant Gaius Fabius and the *quaestor* Marcus Crassus, and after bridges had been speedily constructed, he advanced against the Menapii in three divisions, set fire to their buildings and villages, and seized a large number of cattle and prisoners. This forced the Menapii to send envoys to him to sue for peace. He accepted their hostages and declared that he would treat them as enemies if they admitted either Ambiorix or his envoys within their borders. When these matters had been attended to, he left the Atrebatian, Commius, with a force of cavalry in the territory of the Menapii to keep an eye to them, and he himself proceeded against the Treveri.

CHAPTER 7

WHILE CAESAR WAS ATTENDING to these matters, the Treveri had collected large forces of infantry and cavalry, and were getting ready to attack Labienus and the single legion which was wintering in their territory. They were not more than a two days' march from him, when they learned of the arrival of the two legions which had been sent by Caesar. Therefore they pitched their camp fifteen miles off, and decided to wait for their German auxiliaries. Becoming aware of the design of the enemy and hoping that their rashness might afford him some chance of engaging them, Labienus left five cohorts to guard the baggage, and set out against the enemy with twenty-five cohorts and a large body of cavalry; he pitched camp at a distance of one mile from the enemy. Between Labienus and the enemy was a river with steep banks, which was difficult to cross. He did not intend to cross it himself, and he did not think that the enemy would cross it either. The enemy's hope of auxiliaries was increasing daily. Labienus deliberately declared openly that, since the Germans were said to be approaching, he would not risk his own fortunes and those of the army, and that he would break camp early next day. These words were quickly carried to the enemy, for in a large number of Gallic horsemen it was natural that some should favor the Gallic cause. During the night Labienus summoned the tribunes of the soldiers and the first centurions, and acquainted them with his plan; and in order that he might the more easily give the enemy the impression that he was afraid, he ordered the soldiers to break camp with more noise and disturbance than is customary for Romans. In this way he made his departure look like a flight. Because the camps were so near each other, this too was reported to the enemy by their scouts before the break of day.

CHAPTER 8

HARDLY HAD OUR REAR advanced be-
yond the fortifications when the Gauls began to urge
one another not to let slip through their hands the booty
which they hoped for. Since the Romans were panic-
stricken, it would be wearisome, they said, to wait for
the aid of the Germans; nor would their self-respect
permit them not to dare to attack with such large forces
so small a band, especially when it was fleeing and encumbered with its baggage. Therefore they did not
hesitate to cross the river and to begin the engagement
on unfavorable ground. Labienus had suspected that
this would happen, and to entice them all to cross the
river he feigned a march and calmly advanced forward.
He then sent his baggage a little forward and placed it
upon some rising ground. Then he spoke as follows:
"Soldiers, you have the opportunity you have sought;
you hold the enemy on unfavorable and inaccessible
ground; display under my command the same valor
you have often displayed to the commander-in-chief,
and imagine that he is present and sees our action with
his own eyes." At the same time he commanded the
soldiers to face about towards the enemy and form a
line of battle, dispatched a few squadrons of horsemen
to guard the baggage, and stationed the rest of the
cavalry on the flanks. Our men quickly raised a shout
and hurled their javelins at the enemy. When the enemy unexpectedly saw those whom they believed to be
in flight advancing against them in battle array, they
could not sustain even the first onset, and at the first
charge they fled and sought safety in the neighboring

woods. Labienus pursued them with his cavalry, killed
a great number, took many prisoners, and a few days
later recovered his hold over the tribe. For the Germans, who were coming to the assistance of the Gauls,
returned home when they learned of the flight of the
Treveri. The kinsmen of Indutiomarus, who had been
the instigators of the revolt, followed them out of the
state. The chief civil and military authority of the state
was delivered to Cingetorix, who, as we have shown,
had remained loyal from the beginning.

CHAPTER 9

AFTER CAESAR HAD COME from the ter-
ritory of the Menapii to that of the Treveri, he decided
to cross the Rhine for two reasons: one of these was
that the Germans had sent auxiliaries to the Treveri
against him; the other, to prevent Ambiorix from finding an avenue of retreat among them. Having made
this decision, he proceeded to build a bridge a little
above that place where he had previously led his army
across. Since the plan of such a bridge was familiar
and had been tried, and since the soldiers worked with
much enthusiasm, the work was completed in a few
days. He left a strong guard at the bridge in the territory of the Treveri, to prevent a sudden uprising
among them, and led the rest of the forces and the
cavalry across. The Ubii, who had given hostages before and had surrendered, now, to clear themselves of
any suspicion, sent envoys to him to explain that no
auxiliaries had been sent from their state to the Treveri, and that their pledge had not been violated; they

begged and implored him to spare them, so that in an indiscriminate hatred of the Germans the innocent might not be punished for the guilty; if he wanted more hostages, they promised to give them. Upon further investigation Caesar found out that the auxiliaries had been sent by the Suebi; he therefore accepted the explanation of the Ubii, and made careful inquiry about the approaches and the routes to the country of the Suebi.

CHAPTER 10

MEANWHILE, AFTER A FEW DAYS he was informed by the Ubii that the Suebi were collecting all their forces into one place and ordering the tribes that were under their control to send auxiliaries of infantry and cavalry. When he received this report, he provided for a supply of grain and selected a suitable spot for a camp; he commanded the Ubii to remove their cattle and to bring in all their possessions from the fields into the towns, hoping that uncivilized and inexperienced men, influenced by the lack of provisions, might be induced to fight at a disadvantage; he commanded the Ubii to send a great many scouts into the country of the Suebi and to learn what was going on among them. The Ubii carried out his orders, and after a few days reported that the Suebi, after more trustworthy information had reached them regarding the Roman army, had all withdrawn with all their forces and those of their allies which they had collected, to the most remote part of their country; there was a forest there of immense size called Bacenis; it extended far within and, interposed as a natural barrier, it protected the Cherusci from destructive raids on the part of the Suebi, and the Suebi from raids on the part of the Cherusci; at the entrance to this forest the Suebi had decided to await the coming of the Romans.

CHAPTER 11

SINCE WE HAVE REACHED this point, it does not seem to be out of place to give an account of the customs of Gaul and of Germany, and to explain in what respect they differ from each other. In Gaul, not only in every state and every canton and district, but almost in every family, there are party divisions, and the leaders of these divisions are those men who in the opinion of their fellow citizens are thought to have the greatest influence among them, so that the settlement of all matters and projects is referred to their decision and judgment. That practice seems to have become established in ancient times in order to provide that no man of the common people might lack assistance against a more powerful individual; for no leader would allow the members of his party to be oppressed and defrauded, otherwise he would not enjoy any authority over them. This same condition prevails in general throughout Gaul, for all the states are divided into two groups.

CHAPTER 12

AT THE TIME when Caesar arrived in Gaul, the Aedui were the leaders of one group, the Sequani of the other. Since the latter were less powerful by themselves, inasmuch as the highest authority in former times rested with the Aedui, and their dependencies were great, the Sequani had united with the Germans and Ariovistus, and had won them over by great pecuniary sacrifices and promises. After they had fought several successful battles and slain all the Aeduan nobility, they had so far outstripped the Aedui that they brought over to their side a great part of the dependent states of the Aedui, and received from them as hostages the sons of their leading men. They also compelled their government to take an oath that they would form no hostile designs against the Sequani. They seized by force part of the neighboring territory and retained it in their possession, and secured the leadership of the whole of Gaul. In this extreme situation Diviciacus set out to Rome for the purpose of seeking aid from the Senate; but he returned without accomplishing his object. On Caesar's arrival, a complete change of relations was brought about; their hostages were restored to the Aedui, their old dependencies were won back, new ones were acquired with the help of Caesar, because those who had joined themselves to them as allies saw that they enjoyed a better condition and a more equitable form of government. In all other respects their influence and standing were enhanced, and the Sequani lost their supremacy. The Remi had succeeded to their place; and since it was understood that they stood equally high in Caesar's favor, those who by reason of ancient enmities could by no means join the Aedui attached themselves as dependents to the Remi. These the Remi protected carefully; thus they maintained their new and suddenly acquired authority. At that time the situation was such that the Aedui were considered by far the leading state, and the Remi held the second place of honor.

CHAPTER 13

IN ALL OF GAUL there are two classes of men who are of any account and consideration. The common people are treated almost as slaves; they do not venture to act on their own initiative, and are not invited to any consultation. The greater part of them, oppressed either by debt or heavy taxes, or by the wrongdoing of the more powerful, attach themselves as slaves to the nobles, who have the same rights over them as masters over slaves. Of the two classes mentioned above one consists of Druids, the other of Knights. The former have charge of divine worship, regulate public and private sacrifices, and settle religious questions. A great number of young men come to them in order to receive instruction; the Druids are held in great respect among the Gauls. They generally settle all disputes, both public and private; and if any crime or murder has been committed, if there is any dispute about an inheritance or boundaries, they also render judgment, determining rewards and penalties. If any party to a controversy, whether a private individual or tribe, does not abide by their decision, they

exclude such from the sacrifices. This is the heaviest
penalty among them. Those upon whom such an inter-
dict has been laid are considered as wicked and crime-
polluted men. These all men avoid and shun their approach and conversation, lest they suffer any harm from
contact with them; no justice is rendered them though
they may seek it, no honor is shared with them. One
Druid is in charge of all the others, and he has the
highest authority over them. When he dies, he is succeeded by the Druid who is preeminent in standing; if
there are several of equal standing, they strive for the
headship by the vote of the Druids, and sometimes by
the sword. At a certain time of the year, these Druids
hold a meeting in a hallowed spot in the territory of
the Carnutes, a region which is considered as the center
of all Gaul. To this place come from all quarters those
who have disputes, and they obey the decrees and judg-
ments of the Druids. The system of the Druids is believed to have been discovered in Britain, and from
there to have been brought to Gaul; and now, those
who wish to study the system with special thorough-
ness usually travel to Britain to learn it.

CHAPTER 14

THE DRUIDS USUALLY take no part in
military activity, and do not pay taxes at the same rate
as the rest; they enjoy exemption from military service
and freedom from all public burdens. Attracted by
these great privileges, many come of their own accord
to be trained as Druids, and many others are sent by
their parents and relatives. There they are said to learn

by heart a great number of verses. Therefore some students remain under instruction twenty years. They do not think it proper to commit their teachings to writing, although in almost all other matters, as, for instance, in public and private accounts, they use Greek characters. I suppose that they have adopted this practice for two reasons—in the first place, because they do not wish to have their system spread abroad among the common people, and, in the second place, because they do not wish those who are under instruction to rely on writing, and thus to pay too little heed to the training of their memory; for it usually happens that through reliance upon written records students relax their diligence in learning by heart and impair their memory. They are chiefly anxious to stress the belief that the soul does not die, but passes after death from one body to another; and they think that by this belief men are especially spurred on to courage, since the fear of death has been removed. They also treat many other subjects, such as the stars and their movements, the size of the universe and of the earth, the nature of things, the strength and the power of the immortal gods, and they transmit their knowledge to the young men.

CHAPTER 15

THE SECOND CLASS consists of Knights. Whenever the need arises, or some war breaks out (and before Caesar's arrival it happened almost every year that they would either themselves make attacks or repel those made on them) all these engage in war; of these Knights, the one who is the most distinguished for high birth or wealth has about him the greatest number of vassals and retainers. This is the only form of influence and power that they recognize.

CHAPTER 16

THE GALLIC NATION as a whole is greatly devoted to religious observances; for that reason those who are suffering from rather serious diseases and those who are engaged in dangerous battles either offer up human beings as victims or vow to do so, employing the Druids as officiating priests for these sacrifices. They believe that unless a man's life be given for a man's life, the majesty of the immortal gods may not be appeased; as a state, they have sacrifices of the same kind. Some use figures of immense size, whose limbs, woven out of wickerwork, they fill with living human beings; when these are set on fire, the victims, enveloped by flames, perish. They believe that the execution of those who have been caught in the act of theft or highway robbery, or some other crime, is more acceptable to the immortal gods; but when the supply of such criminals fails, they resort to the execution even of the innocent.

CHAPTER 17

AMONG THE GODS, they worship especially Mercury. There are very many images of this god; they regard him as the inventor of all arts, the guide for roads and journeys, and they believe that he has the greatest influence for the acquisition of money and for commercial transactions. After him come Apollo, Mars, Jupiter, and Minerva. About these deities they have almost the same beliefs as other nations: that Apollo averts disease, Minerva imparts the elements of trades and crafts, Jupiter holds sway over the gods, and Mars controls war. To Mars they generally consecrate the spoils they may win in a battle they have decided to fight. After a victory, they offer up the captured cattle and collect all the other booty into one place. In many states one may see heaps of such objects piled up in hallowed spots; and it seldom happens that a man, disregarding religious obligation, has dared to conceal the captured spoils in his house, or to take away what had been deposited, and the most severe punishment, with torture, has been ordained for such a crime.

CHAPTER 18

THE GAULS ASSERT that they are all descended from Father Dis, and say that this belief has been imparted to them by the Druids. For this reason they measure all divisions of time not by the number of days, but by that of nights; in the observance of birthdays and the beginnings of months and years day follows night. In other customs of life they differ generally from all other peoples; they do not allow their sons to approach them in public until they are old enough to discharge military service, and they consider it disgraceful for a son while still a boy to appear in public in the presence of his father.

CHAPTER 19

THE HUSBANDS APPRAISE the property which they receive from their wives as dowry, and set aside an equivalent amount from their own property and add it to the dowry. A joint account is kept of this common property, and the income is saved; whichever of the two survives, to that person fall the portions of both together with the income of past years. Husbands have the power of life and death over their wives as over their children. When the head of a family, who is of higher rank, dies, his relatives assemble, and if suspicion has arisen regarding the cause of death, they hold a judicial examination of his wives like that of slaves, and if their guilt has been proved, they agonize and kill them with fire and every instrument of torture. Their funerals, considering the civilization of the Gauls, are splendid and costly. They cast into the funeral pyre everything, even animals, which they believe were dear to the deceased in life, and, a little before our time, slaves and dependents known to have been loved by their masters were burned with them at the completion of the regular funeral rites.

CHAPTER 20

THOSE STATES which are considered to manage their public affairs best have it established by law that if anyone has heard from his neighbors by rumor or report anything touching the public interest, he must report it to a magistrate, and must not impart it to anyone else; for it is a known fact that rash and inexperienced men are often frightened by baseless rumors, and so are driven to crime or to the formation of plans of the utmost importance. The magistrates suppress what they think it best to conceal, and make known to the public only what they consider of advantage. No one is allowed to discuss affairs of state anywhere but in a public assembly.

CHAPTER 21

THE GERMANS' MODE of life differs greatly from that of the Gauls. The Germans neither have Druids to preside over divine worship, nor do they pay heed to sacrifices. They regard as gods only those whom they see, and by whose help they are clearly benefited, namely, the Sun, Vulcan, and the Moon; of the other gods they have heard not even by report. Their whole life is spent in hunting and warlike pursuits; from childhood they inure themselves to toil and hardship. Those who remain unmarried for the longest time win greatest praise among their people; they believe that stature, strength, and muscles are promoted by this practice. They consider it most disgraceful to have had relationship with a woman before the twentieth year; there is no secrecy about the matter of sex, for men and women bathe together in rivers, and wear skins or short cloaks of reindeer hide, which leave a great part of the body bare.

CHAPTER 22

THEY SHOW NO INTEREST in farming, and the greater part of their food consists of milk, cheese, and meat. No one has a definite portion of land or estate of his own; the magistrates and chiefs each year assign to clans and groups of families and to those who have joined together as much land as they deem proper and in whatever place they think best, and the following year compel them to move to another place. They offer many reasons for this practice: lest, captivated by the attractiveness of permanent residence, they exchange their eagerness for warlike pursuit for agriculture; that they may not show too great eagerness for the acquisition of large estates, and that the more powerful may not drive the weaker from their possessions; that they may not build houses with too great care as a protection against cold and heat; that there may not arise too great a desire for money, which is the cause of factions and dissensions; that they may keep the common people in a state of contentment, each one seeing that his own wealth is equal to that of the most powerful.

CHAPTER 23

THE STATES REGARD IT as their highest distinction to lay waste their neighboring territory, and thus to have areas of wilderness as far and wide as possible around them. They consider it a proof of valor to drive their neighbors from their fields and to compel them to retire elsewhere, so that no one dares to settle near them; at the same time they think they will be safer after removing the fear of a sudden raid. When a state makes war, or repels an attack that has been made, officers are chosen to conduct that war, and are given the power of life and death. In time of peace they have no such common magistrate, but the chief men of districts and cantons administer justice among their people and settle disputes. Marauding expeditions which are undertaken outside the borders of each state involve no disgrace; the Germans declare that such raids are committed for the purpose of training the young men and of lessening idleness. When a chief announces in an assembly that he is going to be the leader of a raid, and that those who wish to follow him should volunteer, then all those who approve the cause and the man rise, promise their aid, and are highly praised by the assembly. Those who do not follow after volunteering their services are considered as deserters and traitors, and confidence in all matters is afterwards withdrawn from them. They do not think it right to harm a guest; those who have come to them for any cause whatsoever they protect from injury, and regard them as sacred; to them the houses of all are open, and food is shared with them.

CHAPTER 24

THERE WAS A TIME when the Gauls were superior in valor to the Germans, when they actually made war upon them, and because of their large population and the lack of land they sent colonies across the Rhine. And in this way the most productive districts of Germany around the Hercynian forest (I see that this forest was known by report to Eratosthenes and certain Greeks, who called it Orcynia) were seized by the Volcae Tectosages, who settled there; and to this day that tribe continues to maintain itself in these settlements, and has the highest reputation for justice and prowess in war. Now the Germans continue in the same condition of poverty, privation, and hardship as before, and have made no change in their food and clothing. The Gauls, on the other hand, because of their proximity to our provinces and familiarity with products brought across the sea are abundantly supplied with many articles for common use. But since they have gradually become used to being beaten and conquered in many battles, the Gauls do not even compare themselves in valor with the Germans.

CHAPTER 25

THIS HERCYNIAN FOREST, mentioned above, is so wide that it takes an unencumbered traveler nine days to cross it; for in no other way can it be measured, as the people have no system for measuring distances. The forest starts from the frontiers of the Helvetii, the Nemetes, and the Rauraci, and, following the direct line of the Danube, it extends to the frontiers of the Daci and the Anartes; from this point it turns to the left, in a direction away from the river, and because of its size it touches the frontiers of many nations. There is no one in this part of Germany who can say that he has gone to the farthest limit of that forest, though he may have made a journey of sixty days, or who has heard in what place it begins. It is known that many kinds of wild animals not seen in any other places live in that forest; of these the following differ most from other animals and seem worthy of mention.

CHAPTER 26

THERE IS AN OX having the form of a stag, from the middle of whose forehead between the ears projects a single horn, higher and straighter than the horns known to us; at the top, the antler spreads out widely to form, as it were, hands and branches. The natural characteristics of the male and the female are the same, and the shape and the size of the horns are the same.

CHAPTER 27

THERE ARE ALSO ANIMALS which are called elks. Their shape and mottled appearance are like those of goats, but they surpass them slightly in size. Their horns present a broken appearance, their legs are without nodes and joints; they do not lie down to rest, and if any accident has caused them to fall, they cannot get up or lift themselves up. Trees serve them as resting-places; they lean against these, and thus, leaning to one side, they take their rest. When hunters have discovered from the tracks of these animals where they are accustomed to rest, they either undermine all the trees at the roots, or cut into them only so much that they retain perfectly the appearance of standing firm. When the animals, in accordance with their habit, lean against them, with their weight they knock down the weakened trees and they themselves fall down with them.

CHAPTER 28

THERE IS A THIRD SPECIES of those animals; they are called aurochs. These are somewhat smaller than elephants; in appearance, color, and shape they are like bulls. Their strength and speed are great, and they spare neither man nor beast they catch sight of. These the natives trap eagerly in pits, and then kill them. By such arduous exercise the young men develop hardihood, and train themselves by this kind of hunting. Those who have killed the greatest number exhibit the horns in public as evidence of their feat and win high praise. Even if these animals are caught very young, they cannot become domesticated or tamed. Their horns are very different from those of our oxen in size, shape, and appearance. The natives collect them eagerly, mount them with silver at the rim, and at their more elaborate banquets use them as goblets.

CHAPTER 29

WHEN CAESAR HAD LEARNED from the scouts of the Ubii that the Suebi had withdrawn into the forests, he decided not to proceed any farther. For, since all the Germans, as we mentioned above, pay very little attention to agriculture, he feared a scarcity of grain. But that he might not altogether remove from the natives the fear of his return and that he might prevent them from sending reinforcements to the Gauls after he had withdrawn his army, he destroyed for a distance of two hundred feet the farthest section of the bridge which touched the banks of the Ubii, and at the end of the bridge he erected a tower four stories high, and stationed a garrison of twelve cohorts to protect the bridge; he also fortified the station with strong defense works. He placed young Gaius Volcatius Tullus in command of that station and garrison. When the crops were beginning to ripen, he himself set out for the campaign against Ambiorix, through the forest of the Ardennes, which is the largest in all Gaul and extends over five hundred miles in length from the banks of the Rhine and the boundaries of the Treveri to the territory of the Nervii. He sent ahead Lucius Minucius Basilus with all the cavalry to see if he could accomplish anything by a speedy march and by striking at an opportune moment. He instructed him to forbid the lighting of fires in camp so that no information might be conveyed from afar regarding his coming, and said that he would follow immediately.

CHAPTER 30

BASILUS CARRIED OUT Caesar's orders. He completed the march speedily, contrary to the general expectation, and caught many of the enemy in the fields off their guard. Following their directions, he hastened to the place where Ambiorix was reported to be with a few horsemen. Fortune plays a large part in all affairs, and especially in warfare. For it was by a remarkable chance that Basilus came upon Ambiorix himself. When the latter was off his guard and unprepared, Basilus made his appearance before there was any rumor or report of his coming. But it was also by a case of rare good luck that Ambiorix himself escaped alive, after the capture of the entire stock of weapons that he had with him and the seizure of his carriages and horses. This is how it came to pass. His house was in the middle of a forest, as the dwellings of the Gauls usually are (they generally seek the vicinity of woods and rivers in order to escape the heat). Fighting in a confined space, his companions and friends held off the attack of our cavalry for a short time. While these were fighting, one of his men put him on a horse, and the woods concealed his flight. Thus Fortune had great influence in exposing him to danger and in delivering him from it.

CHAPTER 31

IT IS DOUBTFUL whether Ambiorix did not assemble his forces deliberately, because he thought that he ought not to fight a decisive battle, or whether he was prevented from doing so by lack of time and the sudden arrival of our cavalry, since he believed that the rest of the army was following close behind. At all events, he sent messengers in different directions through the country to command every man to look out for his own safety. Some of them fled into the forest of the Ardennes, others into the continuous marshes; those who lived next to the Ocean hid on the islands which the tides are accustomed to form. Many, leaving their own country, entrusted their persons and all their possessions to complete strangers. Catuvolcus, king of half the Eburones, who had entered into the plot with Ambiorix, was now weak and old and unable to endure the hardships of war or flight. Calling down on Ambiorix all manner of curses for having been the instigator of such a scheme, he committed suicide by drinking the juice of the yew, a tree which is very common in Gaul and Germany.

CHAPTER 32

THE SEGNI AND CONDRUSI, two German tribes who live between the Eburones and the Treveri, sent envoys to Caesar to beg him not to regard them as enemies, and not to assume that the Germans who live on this side of the Rhine were all united against him. They declared that they had never planned to make war on him, and had sent no help to Ambiorix. Caesar investigated the matter by an examination of prisoners, and ordered them to bring to him any Eburones who had come to them in their flight; he told them that if they did that, he would not lay waste their territory. Then, having divided his forces into three parts, he collected the baggage of all the legions at Atuatuca. That is the name of a fortress situated almost in the middle of the territory of the Eburones, where Titurius and Aurunculeius had encamped for the winter. He selected this place for several reasons and especially because the fortifications of the previous year remained intact, and this would lighten the labor of the soldiers. To guard the baggage, he left the Fourteenth Legion, one of the three which he had lately enrolled and brought over from Italy. He placed Quintus Tullius Cicero in command of that legion and the camp, and assigned to him two hundred horsemen.

CHAPTER 33

HAVING DIVIDED THE ARMY, he ordered Titus Labienus to proceed with three legions towards the Ocean and those districts which touch the Menapii; he sent Gaius Trebonius with an equal number of legions to lay waste that region which borders upon the country of the Atuatuci; he decided to march himself with the remaining three legions to the river Scheldt, which flows into the Meuse, and to the farthest parts of the Ardennes, where he heard that Ambiorix had gone with a few horsemen. As he was leaving, he declared that he would return in seven days; he knew that by that date the provisions were due to the legion left on guard. He urged Labienus and Trebonius, if they could do it consistently with the public interest, to return by the same day, in order that they might again consult with one another and examine the plans of the enemy so that they could enter the campaign anew.

CHAPTER 34

AS WE MENTIONED ABOVE, the Gauls had no definite force, no stronghold or garrison that was able to defend itself in arms, but they were scattered in all directions. Where a secluded valley or a wooded spot or an impassable marsh offered some hope of defense or safety, there each man had settled. These places were known in their own neighborhood, and this circumstance called for great care, not so much to protect the army as a whole (for no danger could threaten our main body from frightened and scattered individuals) as to ensure the safety of individual soldiers, a consideration which, nevertheless, in some measure concerned the safety of the whole. For the greed for plunder caused many of our men to wander off too far, and the woods prevented them from advancing in close formation along the ill-defined and hidden paths. If Caesar wished to finish off the business and to destroy the race of criminals, he must send more bands in different directions and distribute his soldiers over a wider area, but if he wished to keep the companies with the standards, as the established rule and practice of the Roman army demanded, the hiding-place itself served as a protection to the enemy, among whom individuals did not lack the courage to lay secret ambush and surround our scattered men. In this most difficult situation the greatest possible precautions were taken; although all the soldiers were eager for revenge, Caesar preferred to miss the chance of doing harm to the enemy rather than to do them harm with serious loss to his own men. He sent messengers to the neighboring states and invited them all, in the hope of booty, to join him in plundering the Eburones. He did this so that he might endanger the lives of the Gauls in the forests rather than those of his legionary soldiers, and, at the same time, by surrounding the Eburones with a large number of men, that he might destroy the stock and name of the state as punishment for having committed so great a crime. Large numbers of Gauls soon assembled from all sides.

CHAPTER 35

THESE ACTIVITIES were going on in all parts of the country of the Eburones, and the seventh day was drawing near, on which Caesar had decided to return to the baggage and the legion. Here one may learn how great is the power of luck in war, and how great are the accidents it brings. As the enemy were scattered and scared, as we have mentioned, there was no hostile force that could cause us the slightest alarm. The report reached the Germans across the Rhine that the Eburones were being pillaged, and that everybody was invited to take part in the plunder. Two thousand horsemen were collected by the Sugambri, who live close to the Rhine, by whom, as we mentioned above, the Tencteri and the Usipetes had been received in their flight. They crossed the Rhine on boats and rafts thirty miles below the place where the bridge had been built and a garrison left by Caesar. They arrived at the frontiers of the Eburones, caught many scattered in flight, and seized large herds of cattle, of which barbarians are extremely fond. Lured on by the hope of

more booty, they advanced farther. Neither swamps
nor woods checked these men, born in the midst of war
and brigandage. They inquired of prisoners where Caesar was; they found out that he had advanced farther,
and learned that all his army had departed. And then
one of the prisoners said: "Why do you go after this
miserable and trifling booty, when you have the chance
of becoming most prosperous now? In three hours you
can reach Atuatuca; there the Roman army has deposited all its property; the garrison is so small that
they cannot even man the wall, and no one dares to go
outside the fortifications." Having been offered this
hope, the Germans hid the plunder they had acquired,
and, using as their guide the same man by whose information they had learned these things, they made
straight for Atuatuca.

CHAPTER 36

DURING THE PREVIOUS DAYS, in obedi-
ence to Caesar's instructions, Cicero had most carefully
kept his soldiers in camp, allowing not even a camp
servant to go outside the fortifications. But on the
seventh day he began to doubt whether Caesar would
keep his word regarding the number of days he would
be away, for he heard that he had advanced farther,
and no report about his return was brought to him.
At the same time he was influenced by the remarks of
those who called his patience almost a blockade, since
no one was permitted to go out of the camp. Moreover,
he did not anticipate any accident within three miles of
his camp, when nine legions and a very large force of

cavalry were confronting a scattered and almost annihilated enemy. He therefore sent five cohorts to get
grain in the nearest fields, between which and the camp
there was only a single hill. Many men of the legions
had been left behind sick; those of them who had recovered during the last seven days, about three hundred in number, were sent together as a separate detachment; moreover, a large number of camp servants
were given leave to follow with a large number of
beasts of burden, which had been left in the camp.

CHAPTER 37

AT THIS VERY MOMENT the German
cavalry arrived, and with the same speed they had
come immediately tried to break into the camp by the
rear gate. Because of the woods on that side, they were
not seen until they were near the camp, so much so
that the traders who had their tents at the foot of the
rampart had no chance to escape. Our men, not expect-
ing them, were thrown into confusion by this sudden
attack, and the cohort on guard could hardly sustain
their first assault. The enemy swept around the other
sides, to see if they could find a way in. Our men with
difficulty defended the gates; all other points of entrance were defended by the nature of the place itself
and by the fortifications. There was panic throughout
the camp; the men were asking one another the cause
of the disturbance; nobody knew where an advance
should be made or where each man should fall in. One
announced that the camp was already taken; another
maintained that the Germans had come as victors after

destroying the Roman army and its general. Most of them conceived strange fancies from the place they were in and set before their eyes the disaster of Cotta and Titurius, who, they said, had perished in the same fort. As our men were panic-stricken because of such fears, the Germans were convinced that, as they had heard from the prisoner, there was no garrison inside the camp. They therefore tried hard to break through, encouraging one another not to let so good a chance slip from their hands.

CHAPTER 38

WITH THE GARRISON there had been left behind a sick soldier, Publius Sextius Baculus, first centurion under Caesar, who has been mentioned in connection with previous battles. He had now been without food for five days. Despairing of his own safety and that of all the others, he came out from his tent unarmed. He saw that the enemy were close at hand and that the situation was extremely critical. He snatched arms from the nearest men and stationed himself at the gate. He was followed by the centurions of the cohort on guard; and together for a while they withstood the attack. Sextius was severely wounded, and fainted; with difficulty he was dragged from hand to hand to safety. This respite enabled the rest to pluck up enough courage to dare to take their stations in the fortifications and to make a show of defence.

CHAPTER 39

MEANWHILE, HAVING FINISHED the foraging, our soldiers heard the shouting; the cavalry hastened forward, and learned the seriousness of the situation. But there was no fortification out there to receive the scared soldiers; the lately enrolled soldiers, who were inexperienced in warfare, turned to the tribunes and centurions, waiting to be told what to do. No one was so brave as not to be greatly disturbed by this unexpected situation. The Germans, catching sight of the standards in the distance, gave up their attack on the camp; at first they thought that the legions, which the prisoners had told them had gone farther, had returned; but afterwards, regarding our small numbers with contempt, they attacked them from all sides.

CHAPTER 40

THE CAMP SERVANTS RUSHED forward to the nearest mound. Quickly dislodged from that place, they forced their way in among the soldiers, who were lined up with their standards, thus scaring the frightened soldiers even more. Since the camp was so near, some of the soldiers proposed to form a wedge and break through quickly, feeling confident that even if some of them were surrounded and slain, at least the rest could be saved. Others proposed that they make a stand on the hill and that all meet the same fate together. The veterans, who, as we have shown, had gone out as a separate detachment, did not approve this course. And so they encouraged one another, and, led by Gaius Trebonius, a Roman Knight, who had been put in command of them, they broke through the middle of the enemy and reached camp all safe to a man. They were followed closely in the same charge by the camp servants and the cavalry, who were saved by the valor of the soldiers. But those men who had taken their stand on the ridge showed that they were still un-acquainted with the art of war; they were unable either to stick to the plan which they had approved of defending themselves on higher ground, or to imitate the vigor and the speed which they had seen had helped others; in their attempt to reach the camp, they came down to unfavorable ground. Some of the centurions had been transferred, on account of their bravery, from the lower ranks in other legions to the higher ranks in this legion; these centurions, that they might not lose their previously acquired military glory, fell fighting most bravely. When the enemy had been repulsed by the valor of the centurions, some of the soldiers, though they did not expect it, arrived safely in camp; others were surrounded and killed by the enemy.

CHAPTER 41

BECAUSE THE GERMANS SAW that our men had taken their post in the fortifications, they despaired of storming the camp and retired across the Rhine with the booty which they had hidden in the woods. Even after their departure, so great was the fear of our men that, when Gaius Volusenus, who had been sent ahead with the cavalry, reached the camp that night, he could not convince the soldiers that Caesar was close at hand with his army, safe and sound. Terror had so completely taken possession of them that they almost lost their minds; they declared that after the destruction of all the forces, the cavalry alone managed to flee; they maintained that if our army had been unharmed, the Germans would not have attacked the camp. This terror was removed by the arrival of Caesar.

CHAPTER 42

WHEN CAESAR RETURNED, being not unfamiliar with the vicissitudes of war, he had but one complaint to make—that the cohorts had been sent out of camp away from their outpost and garrison; he said that no room should have been left to even the slightest chance; he concluded that Fortune had shown her great power in the sudden arrival of the enemy, and much more so, in that she had turned away the Germans almost from the very rampart and gates of the camp. The most surprising thing of all was that the Germans, who had crossed the Rhine to lay waste the territory of Ambiorix, had by their attack on the Roman camp rendered Ambiorix the greatest possible service.

CHAPTER 43

CAESAR SET OUT again to harass the enemy; he collected a large force from the neighboring states, and sent them in all directions. All the villages and all the buildings that anyone saw were set on fire;

the captured cattle were driven off from all sides; the crops were not only consumed by the large number of beasts and soldiers, but they were also flattened by the autumn rains. It seemed therefore that even if any Germans succeeded in hiding for the time being, they must die of starvation, after the army had been withdrawn. With so large a force of cavalry scattered in all directions, it often came to pass that the captured prisoners were looking about for Ambiorix, whom they had just seen in flight; they insisted that he had not quite gone out of sight. This raised our men's hopes of catching Ambiorix; by their boundless exertion and almost superhuman efforts they thought they would win the highest favor with Caesar. Yet always success seemed to elude them; Ambiorix made his escape from hiding places or glens, and hiding at night, made for other districts and regions, protected by only four horsemen, to whom alone he dared to entrust his life.

CHAPTER 44

AFTER THE COUNTRY had been laid waste in this way, having lost two cohorts, Caesar led his army to Durocortorum, a city of the Remi; he summoned a council of Gaul at that place, and determined to conduct an investigation regarding the conspiracy of the Senones and Carnutes. Acco, the ringleader of that conspiracy, received a rather heavy sentence; he was flogged to death in the old Roman manner. Some, fearing trial, fled; these were outlawed. Then Caesar stationed in winter quarters two legions on the frontier of the Treveri, two among the Lingones, the remaining six at Agedincum, in the territory of the Senones. After providing a grain supply for the army, he set out for Italy, as he had determined, to hold court.

BOOK VII

CHAPTER 1

SINCE GAUL was now quiet, Caesar, as he had determined, set out for Italy to hold court. There he heard of the murder of Publius Claudius. When he had been informed of the decree of the Senate that all the younger men of military age in Italy should take the military oath, he determined to hold a levy throughout Cisalpine Gaul. These events were rapidly reported to Transalpine Gaul. The Gauls themselves added to the reports and embellished them with rumors as the circumstances of the case seemed to demand, namely, that Caesar was being detained in Italy by the disturbances in Rome and could not, amidst such violent strife, come to his army. Influenced by this favorable opportunity, since even before the Gauls resented their subjection to the power of Rome, they began with greater freedom and daring to form plans for war. The leading men of Gaul summoned meetings in wooded and remote spots, where they complained of the death of Acco, and pointed out that such a fate might happen to all of them. They deplored the common lot of Gaul; by every sort of promise of rewards they earnestly called upon men to start a war and at the risk of their own lives to assert the freedom of Gaul. They said that above all a plan should be de-

vised to cut Caesar off from his army before their secret plans could be divulged. This, they said, was easy
because the legions would not dare to leave their winter quarters in the absence of their general, and the
general could not reach his legions without an escort;
finally, they continued, it was better to be slain in battle than not to be able to recover their ancient renown
in war and the liberty which they had received from
their forefathers.

CHAPTER 2

AFTER THESE MATTERS had been dis-
cussed, the Carnutes declared that they were ready to
face any danger for the sake of the general safety, and
promised that they would be the first of all to make
war; and since at the time they could not give one another pledges of good faith by an exchange of hostages,
for fear that their plans should be made known, they
asked that the compact be ratified by an oath and a
pledge of honor, after their military standards had been
placed close together (in accordance with their custom
this constitutes a most solemn ceremony), to make sure
that they should not be deserted by the rest after they
had started the war. Then all present praised the Carnutes highly, took the oath, and after appointing a day
for commencing hostilities, left the meeting.

CHAPTER 3

WHEN THE APPOINTED DAY came, the Carnutes, under the leadership of two desperate men named Cotuatus and Conconnetodumnus, rushed at a given signal on Cenabum, killed the Roman citizens who had settled there for the purpose of carrying on business (among them Gaius Fufius Cita, a distinguished Roman Knight, who by Caesar's order was in charge of the grain supply), and plundered their property. The report of these events was quickly carried to all the states of Gaul. For whenever any particularly important or remarkable event occurs, the people transmit the news by shouting across the country; others in turn take up the report and pass it on to their neighbors, as happened on this occasion. For although these events had occurred at Cenabum at sunrise, they became known before the end of the first watch in the territory of the Arverni, about one hundred and sixty miles away.

CHAPTER 4

THERE, IN A SIMILAR WAY, Vercingetorix, the son of Celtillus, an Arvernian young man of the highest influence (his father had held the supremacy of all Gaul and had been put to death by the state because he aimed at the kingship), summoned his dependents and easily roused them to revolt. When his design became known, people rushed to arms. His uncle, Gobannitio, and other chiefs who thought that fortune ought not to be tempted in this matter tried to stop him, and expelled him from the town of Gergovia; but he did not give up, and in the fields held a levy of beggars and vagabonds. Having collected such a group of men, he brought over to his side all the men of his state whom he approached; he urged them to take up arms for their common liberty. When he had collected large forces, he drove out of the state his opponents by whom he had been expelled a short time before. He was addressed as "king" by his followers. He sent envoys in every direction, and urged his allies to remain loyal to him. He quickly won over to his side the Senones, Parisii, Pictones, Cadurci, Turoni, Aulerci, Lemovices, Andi, and all the others who border on the Ocean. By general consent, the supreme command was conferred upon him. Having received this power, he demanded hostages from all these states, and ordered a fixed number of soldiers to be brought to him quickly. He determined how great a supply of arms of its own manufacture, and before what time, each state should furnish, and he paid special attention to the cavalry. He maintained not only the utmost care but also the utmost strictness of discipline; by severity of punishment he brought over to his side those who hesitated to join him. For the commission of a rather serious crime he put the criminal to death with fire and all sorts of torture; for a slight offence he sent the offenders home with their ears cut off or one eye gouged out, to serve as a warning to the rest and to frighten others by the severity of the punishment.

CHAPTER 5

HAVING SPEEDILY RAISED an army by these punishments, he sent Lucterius, a Cadurcan of the utmost daring, with a part of the forces into the territory of the Ruteni, and he himself set out against the Bituriges. On his arrival the Bituriges sent envoys to the Aedui, under whose protection they were, to ask for aid in order that they might more easily resist the forces of the enemy. On the advice of the lieutenants whom Caesar had left with the army, the Aedui sent forces of cavalry and infantry to aid the Bituriges. When they came to the Loire, which separates the Bituriges from the Aedui, they delayed there several days. Not daring to cross the river, they returned home, and reported to our lieutenants that they had returned because of the fear of treachery on the part of the Bituriges, who, they had learned, had planned, if the Aedui crossed the river, to surround them on one side, while the Arverni surrounded them on the other. As it is not at all clear to us whether they did this for the reason which they gave to the lieutenants, or from motives of treachery, it does not seem right to make a positive statement. Upon their departure, the Bituriges immediately joined the Arverni.

CHAPTER 6

THESE MATTERS WERE REPORTED to Caesar in Italy; since he understood that affairs in Rome had been brought to a more favorable state by the energetic action of Gnaeus Pompey, he therefore set out for Transalpine Gaul. When he came there, he experienced great difficulty in devising a plan for reaching his army. For if he should summon the legions to the Province, he realized that they would have to fight on the march without him; if, on the other hand, he should try to make his way to the army himself, he saw that it was not wise to entrust his safety at so critical a time even to those who seemed to be at peace.

CHAPTER 7

MEANWHILE LUCTERIUS the Cadurcan, who had been sent into the country of the Ruteni, won over that state to the Arverni. He then proceeded into the country of the Nitiobroges and the Gabali and received hostages from both, and, after collecting a large force, he hastened to make a raid on the Province in the direction of Narbo. When this was reported, Caesar thought that setting out for Narbo should precede all other plans. When he came there, he encouraged the frightened inhabitants, placed garrisons among the Ruteni in the Province, the Volcae Arecomici, the Tolosates, and in the localities around Narbo which were close to the enemy. He ordered a part of the forces of the Province and the raw contingent which he had brought from Italy to assemble in the territory of the Helvii, which touches the territory of the Arverni.

CHAPTER 8

AS A RESULT of these measures, Lucterius was checked and forced to retire, because he deemed it dangerous to enter the chain of our garrisons; Caesar therefore set out into the country of the Helvii. The mountain range Cebenna, which separates the Arverni from the Helvii, during the inclement season of the year hindered our march because all the passes were covered with very deep snow. But the snow was cleared away to a depth of six feet and the roads were opened up by the utmost effort on the part of the soldiers; this made it possible for Caesar to reach the territory of the Arverni. They were caught off their guard, for they thought themselves protected by Mount Cebenna as if by a wall (not even for a single traveler had the mountain trails ever been passable at that season of the year). He ordered the cavalry to spread out as far as possible and to strike the greatest possible terror into the enemy. These events were quickly announced to Bercingetorix by report and messages; all the Arverni crowded around him in alarm, and entreated him to look out for their property and not to let them be plundered by the enemy, especially since he saw that the whole war had been turned against them. Influenced by their entreaties, he moved his camp from the country of the Bituriges in the direction of that of the Arverni.

CHAPTER 9

BUT CAESAR DELAYED two days in this place because he had anticipated that these movements on the part of Vercingetorix would take place; he then left the army on the pretext of bringing together his new force and the cavalry. He placed young Brutus in command of these forces, and instructed him to have his cavalry range as far as possible in every direction; he said that he would try not to be away from the camp longer than three days. Having arranged these matters, he reached Vienna by forced marches even to the surprise of his own men. There he found a fresh contingent of cavalry, which he had sent ahead to that place many days before, and without interrupting his march by day or night, he pushed forward through the territory of the Aedui into that of the Lingones, where two legions were wintering, so that, if any plan involving his personal safety should be entertained by the Aedui, he might forestall it by quickness of movement. When he arrived there, he sent word to the rest of the legions, and assembled all of them in one place before any report of his arrival could reach the Arverni. When Vercingetorix was informed of this, he led his army back to the country of the Bituriges, and starting from there, he determined to attack Gorgobina, a town of the Boii, whom Caesar had settled there after defeating them in the war with the Helvetii, and had made subject to the Aedui.

CHAPTER 10

THIS MOVEMENT of Vercingetorix caused Caesar great difficulty in the formation of his plan of action. If he kept his legions in one place for the rest of the winter, he was afraid that, if the dependents of the Aedui were subdued, the whole of Gaul would revolt, since it saw that Caesar could offer no protection to his friends. But if he led the legions out of their winter quarters too soon, he was afriad that he would be troubled by the lack of grain on account of difficulties of transportation. However, it seemed better to endure every difficulty rather than by acquiescing in so great an indignity to alienate the good will of all those who were loyal to him. Therefore he exhorted the Aedui to supply him with provisions, and sent men ahead to the Boii to inform them of his coming and to urge them to remain loyal and to resist the attack of the enemy with great courage. Leaving two legions and the baggage of the entire army at Agedincum, he set out for the country of the Boii.

CHAPTER 11

NEXT DAY HE ARRIVED at Vellaunodunum, a town of the Senones; in order to leave no enemy in his rear and have readier access to his grain supply, he determined to besiege the town, and in two days surrounded it with entrenchments. On the third day envoys were sent from the town to discuss terms of surrender; Caesar ordered them to collect their arms

in one place, to bring forth their beasts of burden, and
to give six hundred hostages. He left the lieutenant
Gaius Trebonius to see to the execution of these orders.
In order to complete his march as soon as possible, he
himself set out for Cenabum, a town of the Carnutes.
The news of the siege of Vellaunodunum had been
brought to the Carnutes; thinking that the siege would
be prolonged, they were getting ready a garrison to
send to Cenabum for the purpose of defending it. Caesar arrived there in two days. He pitched his camp before the town, but he was prevented by the late hour
of the day from further action; he therefore put off the
attack to the following day. He ordered the soldiers to
prepare everything necessary for the assault; and as a
bridge over the Loire extended to the town of Cenabum, he feared that its inhabitants might escape from
the town by night, and therefore ordered two legions
to keep watch under arms. A little before midnight the
inhabitants of Cenabum moved out silently from the
town and began to cross the river. When this was reported to Caesar by scouts, he set the gates on fire,
sent in the legions which he had ordered to be ready
for action, and took possession of the town. Very few
of the enemy escaped capture, because the narrow
bridge and roads had prevented the escape of so large
a crowd. He plundered and burned the town, gave the
booty to his soldiers, led his army across the Loire,
and reached the territory of the Bituriges.

CHAPTER 12

WHEN VERCINGETORIX HEARD of Caesar's approach, he raised the siege of Gorgobina and set out to meet him. Caesar had begun to assault Noviodunum, a town of the Bituriges, situated on his line of march. When envoys came to him from the town to beg that he pardon them and spare their lives, in order that he might complete the remainder of the campaign as speedily as he had completed most of the previous ones, he ordered their arms to be collected in one place, their horses to be brought forth, and hostages to be given. When a part of the hostages had already been handed over, and the other orders were being carried out, and when some centurions and a few soldiers had been sent into the town to collect the arms and beasts of burden, the cavalry of the enemy, which had preceded the army of Vercingetorix, was seen at a distance. As soon as the inhabitants caught sight of them and came to entertain the hope of assistance, they raised a shout and began to take up their arms, to shut the gates, and to man the wall. When the centurions in the town realized from the behavior of the Gauls that they were planning some new mischief, they seized the gates with drawn swords, and withdrew all their men in safety.

CHAPTER 13

CAESAR ORDERED THE CAVALRY to be brought out of camp, and engaged the enemy in a cavalry battle. When his men were hard pressed, he sent to their aid about four hundred German horsemen, whom from the beginning of the Gallic war he had been accustomed to keep with him. The Gauls could not resist their attack, and having been put to flight, they retreated to their main body after losing many of their men. When these had been routed, the townsmen, once more panic-stricken, seized those by whose efforts they thought the people had been roused, brought them to Caesar, and surrendered to him. When this part of the campaign had been finished, Caesar set out to Avaricum, the largest and best fortified town in the territory of the Bituriges, situated in the most fertile district of the country, because he felt sure that by the capture of that town he would bring the state of the Bituriges into his power.

CHAPTER 14

HAVING SUFFERED so many successive defeats, at Vellaunodunum, Cenabum, and Noviodunum, Vercingetorix summoned his men to a council of war. He pointed out that the war must be waged in a fashion far different from that which they had previously used. They must try by every means to prevent the Romans from obtaining forage and supplies. This was easy because the Gauls were strong in cavalry and were aided by the time of the year. The grass could not be cut; the enemy must necessarily scatter and seek it in the barns; all these scattered parties could be destroyed daily by the cavalry. Moreover, private interests must be sacrificed for the benefit of the general safety. In every direction villages and isolated buildings must be burned for as great a distance from the Romans' route as they seemed capable of reaching in search of forage. They themselves had a supply of these necessities, because they were aided by the resources of those in whose territory the war was being carried on. The Romans would either be unable to endure the lack of provisions, or would advance farther from their camp at great risk; and it made no difference whether they killed them or stripped them of their baggage, without which they could not carry on a war. Furthermore, any towns which were not safe from all danger by their fortifications or by the nature of their position ought to be burned, in order that they might not serve as a refuge for their own countrymen for shirking military service, nor prove handy to the Romans for carrying off quantities of provisions and booty. If these measures seemed grievous or harsh, they ought to consider that it was far more grievous that their children and their wives should be carried off into slavery, and that they themselves should be slain; this would surely happen to them if they were conquered.

CHAPTER 15

THIS PROPOSAL WAS APPROVED by unamous consent, and in a single day more than twenty towns of the Bituriges were set on fire. The same thing was done in the other states, and fires were seen in every direction; although all bore this with great pain, yet they consoled themselves with the thought that by an almost assured victory they would quickly recover their losses. The question whether Avaricum should be burned or defended was discussed in a general assembly. The Bituriges threw themselves at the feet of all the Gauls and begged them that they should not be compelled to set fire with their own hands to a city that was perhaps the most beautiful in all Gaul, the protection and the ornament of the state. They said that they would easily defend it because of its natural situation, for on almost all sides it was surrounded by the river and the marsh, and had but one very narrow approach. Their petition was granted. Vercingetorix opposed it at first, but afterwards consented, in consequence of their prayers and of the compassion of the general body. Capable defenders were chosen for the town.

CHAPTER 16

VERCINGETORIX FOLLOWED Caesar by easy stages, and chose for his camp a site protected by marshes and woods, at a distance of sixteen miles from Avaricum. There by organized patrols he was informed hourly what was going on about Avaricum, and gave orders for what he desired done. He was constantly on the watch for our men going out for fodder and grain, and when they were scattered and were obliged to advance any distance, he would attack them and inflict heavy losses upon them; our men, as far as they could provide against this by strategy, met the emergency by going out at irregular intervals and by different routes.

CHAPTER 17

CAESAR PITCHED HIS CAMP on that side of the town which was left open by the river and the marshes and had, as we mentioned above, a narrow approach. He proceeded to build a rampart, to bring up sheds, and to erect two towers, for the nature of the locality prevented him from investing the town. He did not stop asking the Boii and the Aedui to send grain; the latter, because they were acting without enthusiasm, did not help him much, and the former, having no great resources, because their state was small and weak, quickly used up what they had. So the army was in very serious difficulties with regard to its grain supply because of the poverty of the Boii, the indifference of the Aedui, and the burning of the granaries, even to such a degree that for several days the soldiers were without grain and warded off extreme famine by driving in cattle from more distant villages. Yet not a word was heard from them that was unworthy of the dignity of the Roman people and of their former victories. Indeed, when Caesar addressed separate legions at their work and said that if they felt the scarcity of grain too keenly he would raise the siege, they all with one voice begged him not to do so. They had served, they said, for many years under his command without ever disgracing themselves, without ever failing to accomplish their purpose. They would consider it a disgrace if they abandoned the siege they had begun; it would be better to endure any hardship than to fail to avenge the Roman citizens who had perished at Cenabum by the treachery of the Gauls. They expressed the same opinion to the centurions and military tribunes with the request that they report it to Caesar.

CHAPTER 18

WHEN THE TOWERS had been moved up to the wall, Caesar learned from prisoners that Vercingetorix had used up his forage, had moved his camp nearer Avaricum, and that he himself had gone forward with his cavalry and light-armed infantry, which usually fought with the cavalry, to set an ambush in the place where he thought our troops would go next day to get forage. Having learned this, Caesar set out in silence at midnight, and reached the camp of the enemy in the morning. But having speedily learned through their scouts of Caesar's arrival, they hid their wagons and baggage in the denser parts of the woods, and drew up all their forces on a high open spot. When this was reported to Caesar, he ordered the soldiers to pile up their packs and get their arms ready for action.

CHAPTER 19

THERE WAS A HILL with a slight upward slope from the bottom, which was surrounded on almost every side by a dangerous and impassable marsh, not more than fifty feet wide. The Gauls had broken down the causeways over the marsh and posted themselves on this hill in full confidence in their position; distributed according to their tribes, they held all the fords and thickets close to that marsh. They were firmly determined, if the Romans tried to force their way through the marsh, to overwhelm them from the higher ground when they were stuck fast in the swamp. If one noted the proximity of the two forces, he would think that the Gauls were ready to fight on an almost equal footing; but if anyone observed the inequality of the conditions, he would realize that the Gauls were showing off, and that their display of courage was but a mere sham. Our soldiers were indignant that the enemy could face them at such close range, and demanded the signal for battle. But Caesar told them that a victory on this occasion must necessarily involve great loss and the sacrifice of many brave men. He said that when he saw them determined to face any danger for his glory, he would be guilty of the greatest injustice if he did not hold their lives dearer than his reputation. Having thus comforted his soldiers, he led them back to camp the same day, and began to get ready whatever was necessary for the siege of the town.

CHAPTER **20**

WHEN VERCINGETORIX returned to his
men, he was accused of treachery, because he had
moved the camp nearer the Romans, because he had
gone off with all the cavalry, because he had left so
large a force without a commander, and because on his
departure the Romans had come so opportunely with
such speed. All this could not have happened by chance
or without design; he preferred, they said, to hold the
kingship of Gaul by the favor of Caesar rather than as
their gift. Accused in such a manner, he replied to the
charges as follows: He had moved camp because of the
shortage of fodder and actually at their own request; he
had gone nearer the Romans because he had been influenced by the favorable nature of the ground, which
could defend itself by its own fortification; moreover,
the service of the cavalry should not have been missed
on marshy ground, and it had been useful in the place
to which it had gone. He had intentionally given the
chief command to no one when he departed for fear
that the person chosen might be driven by the zeal of
the soldiers to an engagement, for which he saw that
all were eager because of their irresolute spirit, as they
could no longer endure hardship. If the Romans appeared on the scene by chance, the Gauls ought to feel
grateful to chance; if they had been summoned there
by someone's information, they should feel grateful to
the informer for having enabled them to learn from the
higher position the small number of the Romans, and
to despise the courage of those who did not dare to
fight, but had retreated disgracefully to their camp. He

had no wish to obtain from Caesar by treachery the power which he could have by a victory already assured to himself and to all the Gauls. Moreover, he gave back the command to them if they thought they were bestowing honor on him rather than receiving security from him. "That you may see," he said, "that what I say is true, listen to Roman soldiers." He then brought forward slaves whom he had caught while they were foraging a few days before and whom he had tortured with hunger and chains. These had been previously told what to state when questioned, and now said that they were legionary soldiers; induced by hunger and want, they had secretly left the camp to see if they could find any grain or cattle in the fields; the whole army was suffering from similar want, no one had any strength left, and no one could bear the strain of work; therefore, they concluded, the general had decided, if they made no progress with the siege of the town, to withdraw the army in three days. "These are the benefits," said Vercingetorix, "you have from me, whom you accuse of treachery; by my effort, without the shedding of a drop of your blood, you see a great and victorious army almost destroyed by starvation; I have seen to it that when this army retreats in disgraceful flight, no state shall admit it into its territory."

CHAPTER 21

THE WHOLE CROWD raised a shout, and clashed their arms according to their custom, as they usually do in the case of a man whose speech they approve. They declared that Vercingetorix was a very great leader, that there could be no doubt of his loyalty, and that the war could not be carried on with greater skill. They decided that ten thousand men picked from the entire army should be sent into the town, and thought that the general safety should not be entrusted to the Bituriges alone, since they realize that if the Bituriges alone saved the town, they would claim all credit for the ultimate triumph.

CHAPTER 22

THE EXCEPTIONAL COURAGE of our soldiers was matched by devices of every sort used by the Gauls; for they are a nation gifted with the greatest skill, and extremely apt to copy and develop ideas suggested to them by anyone. They turned aside our grappling hooks with nooses, and when they had grasped them firmly, drew them inside the town with windlasses; they also tried to undermine our terrace, all the more skilfully because they have large iron mines in their country, and every kind of mine is known and familiar to them. Moreover, they had covered the whole wall on every side with towers furnished with platforms, and covered them with hides. Then in frequent sallies by day and night they tried to set fire to our terrace or to attack our soldiers engaged in the work; and by joining the poles together on their own towers and providing them with floors, they brought their towers to a level with ours, whose height was raised by daily additions to the terrace; they tried to impede the work on the exposed ends of the passages of our mines by throwing into them stakes burned and sharp-

ened at the ends, boiling pitch, and very heavy stones.
They thus tried to prevent their approach to the walls.

CHAPTER 23

ALL GALLIC WALLS are generally built
on the following plan. Beams are laid on the ground at
equal intervals of two feet at right angles to the proposed structure, in unbroken succession along the
length of the wall. These are fastened together on the
inside and covered with much rubble, but the intervals
mentioned above are closely packed in front with big
stones. When these beams have been placed and fastened together, a second course is added above, in such
a way that the same interval of two feet is kept and the
beams do not touch one another, but at equal spaces
apart the different beams are held in position by stones
tightly laid in between. In this way the whole wall is
constructed step by step until the proper height of
the wall is reached. This structure is not unsightly
in its diversified appearance, with alternate beams and
stones which keep their courses in straight lines; its
construction is eminently suitable for the defense of
cities, since the stone protects it from fire, and the timber from the battering-ram, for, made fast on the inside with continuous beams, generally forty feet long,
it can neither be broken to pieces nor wrenched asunder.

CHAPTER 24

THE SIEGE WAS IMPEDED by all these measures; although the soldiers were delayed all the time by the cold and the incessant rains, still by unremitting effort they overcame all these obstacles, and in twenty-five days they built a ramp three hundred and thirty feet wide and eighty feet high. When it almost touched the enemy's wall, and Caesar, as was his custom, was watching the work and was urging the soldiers not to stop working even for a moment, a little before the third watch it was discovered that smoke was rising from the ramp, which the enemy had undermined and had set on fire. At the same time all along the wall a shout was raised by the Gauls, and a sortie was made by them from two gates, on either side of our towers. Others, at a distance, were hurling firebrands and dry wood from the wall on to the terrace, and poured down pitch and other inflammable material, so that it was hardly possible to decide where the soldiers should rush first, or to what part assistance should be brought. However, as in accordance with Caesar's practice two legions were always on guard before the camp, and larger numbers were engaged on the siege works by turns, it was speedily arranged that some check the sorties, others pull back the towers and cut the siege embankment in two, and that the whole force rush from the camp to put out the fire.

CHAPTER 25

THERE WAS FIGHTING everywhere for the rest of the night, and the enemy's hope of victory was constantly renewed, all the more so because they saw that the breastworks of the towers were burned, and noticed that the soldiers exposed to the enemy's missiles could not easily come forward to help, while in their own ranks fresh men were continually relieving the weary; they believed that the safety of Gaul depended on that very moment. Then there happened before our eyes something which, as it seems worth telling, we must not fail to mention. Before the gate of the town a Gaul was hurling into the flames opposite one of our towers lumps of tallow and pitch that were passed along to him. His right side was pierced by a dart from a scorpion and he fell down dead. One of the men next to him, stepping over his prostrate body, took over his job; and when this second man was killed in the same fashion by a dart from a scorpion, a third took his place, and a fourth succeeded the third; and that place was not abandoned by the defenders until the fire on the siege embankment was extinguished, the enemy was driven back on all sides, and an end was made to the fighting.

CHAPTER 26

THE GAULS HAD TRIED everything, and, as nothing had succeeded, the next day at the exhortation and order of Vercingetorix they decided to flee from the town. They hoped that by attempting flight in the stillness of the night they might accomplish it with no great loss of their men, since the camp of Vercingetorix was not far from the town, and the marsh which lay without a break between the town and the Romans would delay our pursuit. Now night had come, and they were preparing to do this, when the matrons suddenly rushed out into the streets, and, casting themselves in tears at the feet of their husbands, begged them fervently not to surrender them and their children to the enemy for punishment, since natural weakness prevented them from taking flight. When they saw that their husbands stood firm in their purpose, for generally in extreme peril fear knows no pity, they began to cry out together and to give notice to the Romans of their husbands' intended flight. Frightened by this and fearing that the roads might be seized in advance by the Roman cavalry, they gave up their design.

CHAPTER 27

THE NEXT DAY, when a tower had been moved forward and the siege works which Caesar had begun to construct were finished, a heavy rain came on. Caesar thought this storm suitable for carrying out his plan, because he noticed that the guards on the wall had been posted rather carelessly. He therefore ordered his men to go about their work less energetically, and told them what he wanted done. The legions within the sheds secretly got ready for action. Caesar urged them to reap the fruit of victory at long last as a reward for their great labors; he offered prizes to those who should be the first to mount the wall, and gave the signal for attack to the soldiers. They dashed forward suddenly from all sides and swiftly lined the wall.

CHAPTER 28

THE ENEMY were panic-stricken by the strange maneuver, and when they were dislodged from the wall and towers, they made a stand in wedge-shaped masses in the market place and the more open places, determined to draw up their line and fight it out if an attack should be made from any quarter. When they saw that no one was coming down to level ground and that the Romans distributed themselves thickly all along the wall, they feared that the hope of flight might be cut off altogether. They therefore threw down their arms and without a pause ran to the farthest parts of the town. There, as they blocked their own way at the narrow passage through the gates, some were slain by the soldiers, others who had gotten out of the gates were slain by the cavalry. No one of our soldiers was eager for booty. Enraged by the massacre at Cenabum and the toll occasioned by the siege, the soldiers spared neither the aged, nor the women, nor the children. In short, out of the whole number, which was about forty thousand, scarcely eight hundred, who at the first alarm had rushed out of the town, reached Vercingetorix in safety. He took them in late at night in silence. But fearing that a mutiny might arise in camp if they were met and pitied by the rank and file, he stationed his friends and leading men of the different states along the road at a distance from the camp, with orders to separate the fugitives and conduct them to their friends in the part of the camp that had from the first been assigned to each state.

CHAPTER 29

THE NEXT DAY, calling a council of war, Vercingetorix comforted his men, and exhorted them not to lose heart altogether, nor to be upset by the disaster. The Romans, he said, had not conquered by courage or in pitched battle, but by some cunning and by skill in siege operations, in which the Gauls had no experience. Those were in error who expected in war nothing but success. He himself had never approved the defense of Avaricum; of that he had the Gauls themselves as witnesses. This disaster had been brought about by the lack of foresight of the Bituriges and the too ready acquiescence of the rest. However, he would speedily remedy it by greater successes. By his own efforts he would win over to their side the states which disagreed with the rest of the Gauls, and bring about a combined plan of action for the whole of Gaul, whose unanimous effort not even the whole world could resist; and he had almost brought this about. Meanwhile it was proper that they should be prevailed on for the common good to proceed to fortify the camp, in order that they might more easily resist sudden attacks of the enemy.

CHAPTER 30

THIS SPEECH was not displeasing to the Gauls, chiefly because the general had not lost heart after suffering so great a disaster and had not withdrawn into hiding and shunned their gaze. He was considered to possess greater foresight and forethought, because, while all was yet well, he had at first been of the opinion that Avaricum should be burned, and afterwards that it should be abandoned. And so, although reverses as a rule diminish the authority of commanders, the prestige of Vercingetorix, on the contrary, was enhanced every day that followed the disaster. At the same time, by reason of his assurance, they began to entertain the hope of winning the other states over to their side; and now, for the first time, the Gauls began to fortify their camp, and they were so strengthened in spirit that, though unused to hard work, they thought that they must submit to any and all commands.

CHAPTER 31

TRUE TO HIS WORD, Vercingetorix strove with all his might to win over the other states, and did his best to attract them by presents and promises. For this purpose he selected best qualified persons, each of whom, either by subtle words or by friendly association, could win them over most easily. Those who had escaped after the fall of Avaricum he had provided with arms and clothing; at the same time, to strengthen the diminished forces, he levied a definite number of soldiers upon the states, stating how many he wanted and on what day they should be brought into camp; and he ordered all archers, of whom there was a very large number in Gaul, to be sought out and sent to him. By these measures he quickly made up the losses that had been suffered at Avaricum. Meanwhile, Teutomatus, the son of Ollovico, king of the Nitiobriges, whose father had been called "Friend" by the Roman Senate, came to Vercingetorix with a large number of cavalry from his own state and others whom he had hired in Aquitania.

CHAPTER 32

CAESAR STAYED several days at Avaricum; there he found an immense supply of grain and other provisions, with which the soldiers recovered their strength after their toil and lack of food. It was now near the end of winter; the very season invited Caesar to resume the war; he therefore decided to march against the enemy to see if he could either entice them out of the marshes and woods or blockade them. At this very time some of the leading men of the Aedui came as envoys to ask him to aid their state at a most urgent crisis. The situation, they said, was in the utmost peril. Of old it had been their practice to elect a single magistrate to hold sovereign power for a year; but now there were two such magistrates in office, each of whom claimed to have been legally elected. One of the two was Convictolitavis, an influential and distinguished young man; the other was Cotus, a descendant of a very old house, a man of great power and wide family connections, whose brother Valetiacus had held the same office the year before. The whole state was up in arms; the senate and the people were divided, each claimant had his own backers. If the quarrel were kept up much longer, the result would be that one half of the state would be at war with the other half. Only Caesar's energy and authority could prevent this.

CHAPTER 33

CAESAR THOUGHT it might be detrimental for him to leave the fighting front and the enemy, but he knew what serious troubles generally arise from such disputes. In order to prevent so large a state, so closely connected with the Roman people (a state which he himself had always fostered and by every means honored) from resorting to violence and arms, and in order to prevent that party which had the least confidence in itself from seeking assistance from Vercingetorix, he thought it was his duty to attend to this matter first. And since, in accordance with the laws of the Aedui, the chief magistrate was not permitted to leave the country, in order that he might not seem to have slighted their rights or their laws, Caesar determined to go there in person. He summoned their entire senate and those who were engaged in the quarrel to join him at Decetia. Almost the whole state assembled there, and Caesar was informed that in a small and secret assembly, held neither in the proper place nor at the proper time, Cotus had been declared elected by his brother, although the laws forbade two persons of one family to be elected to the magistracy or even to sit in the senate, while the person previously elected was still living. Caesar therefore made Cotus resign his office, and told Convictolitavis, who according to the custom of the country had been elected by the priests when the magistracy was vacant, to continue in office.

CHAPTER 34

HAVING SETTLED this matter, he urged the Aedui to forget their disputes and quarrels, and, putting aside everything else, to devote their attention to the present war, looking forward to receiving from him the rewards they deserved upon the completion of the conquest of Gaul. He asked them to send him immediately all their cavalry and ten thousand infantry, so that he might distribute them in various garrisons for the protection of the corn supply. He then divided his army into two parts: four legions he assigned to Labienus and instructed him to lead them against the Senones and the Parisii, and six he led himself along the river Allier towards the town of Gergovia, in the country of the Arverni; he assigned part of the cavalry to Labienus, part he kept himself. On learning this, Vercingetorix destroyed all the bridges over that river and began to march along the opposite bank.

CHAPTER 35

THE TWO OPPOSING ARMIES had proceeded along the opposite banks, when Vercingetorix pitched his camp in sight of and almost opposite Caesar's camp, posting scouts about to prevent the Romans from constructing a bridge anywhere and leading their forces across. Caesar found himself in a very difficult position; he feared that he would be blocked by the river for the greater part of the summer, since the Allier is not usually fordable before the autumn. To prevent this, he pitched camp in a wooded spot opposite one of the bridges which Vercingetorix had caused to be destroyed, and next day he stayed there in concealment with two legions, sending on the rest of the army as usual with all the baggage, with some of the cohorts spread out so as to make it appear that the number of the legions remained unchanged. He commanded them to march on as far as they could, and when from the time of the day he inferred that they were safe in camp, he began to rebuild the bridge on the original piles, the lower parts of which were still intact. The work was quickly completed and the legions were led across. Then, choosing a suitable site for a camp, he recalled the rest of the army. When Vercingetorix heard of it, he moved ahead by forced marches, in order that he might not be compelled to fight against his will.

CHAPTER 36

FROM HERE AFTER A MARCH of five
days Caesar reached Gergovia; on the day of his arrival
he fought a slight cavalry skirmish and reconnoitred
the position of the city. As it was situated on a very
high mountain and the approaches to it were difficult
on every side, he despaired of a successful assault. He
therefore decided not to attempt a siege until he had arranged for his grain supply. Vercingetorix had pitched
camp near the town, and had stationed the forces of the
various states separately at short distances around his
quarters; they occupied all the elevations of that ridge,
from which a view over the plain could be had, and
presented a formidable appearance. He ordered the
chieftains of the states, whom he had chosen as his
council of war, to assemble at dawn daily at his quarters to exchange intelligence or make arrangements;
and he allowed hardly a day to pass without testing
each man's courage and fighting spirit by means of a
cavalry skirmish with archers placed among them. Opposite the town there was a hill at the very foot of the
mountain, strongly fortified by nature and precipitous
on all sides; if our men could occupy this, they thought
that they could cut the enemy off from a considerable
part of their water supply and from freedom of foraging; but this place was held by the enemy, though with
an inadequate force. Nevertheless, Caesar marched out
of camp in the dead of night, and, before relief could
come from the town, he dislodged the garrison, took
possession of the place, and there stationed two legions. He then constructed two parallel trenches, each

twelve feet wide, from the greater to the lesser camp, so that men could go to and fro, even one at a time, safe from sudden attack of the enemy.

CHAPTER 37

WHILE THESE EVENTS were taking place at Gergovia, the Aeduan Convictolitavis, to whom, as mentioned above, the magistracy had been awarded by Caesar, was bribed by the Arverni. He entered into negotiations with some young men, whose leaders were Litaviccus and his brothers, young men of a very distinguished family. He shared the bribe with them, and urged them to remember that they were free men and born to rule. The state of the Aedui alone, he said, stood in the way of absolutely certain Gallic victory; by its influence the other states were kept from rising; if it were won over, the Romans would have no foothold in Gaul. To be sure, he continued, he had received some benefit from Caesar, but only to the extent that he had been sustained in a perfectly just claim, but the cause of national liberty was his first duty. Why should the Aedui come to Caesar to adjudicate questions regarding their legal rights, rather than have the Romans come to the Aedui? The young men were quickly won over by the speech of Convictolitavis and by the bribe; they declared that they would be the very first to support the enterprise. They then sought a way of carrying out their plan, since they did not feel sure that the state could be induced to undertake a war without some good reason. It was decided that Litaviccus should be put in command of the ten

thousand soldiers who were on the point of being sent
to Caesar for the war, that he should direct their
march, and that his brothers should hurry on ahead to
Caesar. They also planned how to carry out the remainder of their scheme.

CHAPTER 38

LITAVICCUS TOOK OVER the army, and
when he was about thirty miles from Gergovia, he suddenly called together his soldiers, and with tears in his
eyes he addressed them as follows: "Soldiers, where are
we going? All our cavalry and all our men of high rank
have perished. Two leading citizens of our state,
Eporedorix and Viridomarus, have been accused of
treachery by the Romans and put to death without a
hearing. Learn the facts from those men who escaped
that massacre; for my brothers and all my other relatives have been put to death, and grief prevents me
from telling what happened there." The persons
whom he had told what he wished them to say were
brought forward, and they told the troops the same
story which Litaviccus had told: that many horsemen
of the Aedui had been put to death because it was al-
leged that they had entered into negotiation with the
Arverni; that they themselves had hidden in the crowd
of soldiers and escaped from the midst of the slaughter.
The Aedui raised a shout and begged Litavicus to
provide for their safety. "As if," said he, "this were a
matter for deliberation, and it were not absolutely
necessary for us to march straight to Gergovia and
unite with the Arverni. Can we doubt that after com-

mitting an atrocious crime the Romans are even now
hastening here to kill us too? So, if we have any courage left, by slaying these ruffians let us avenge the
death of those who died most shamefully." He then
pointed to some Roman citizens who were accompany-
ing him in reliance on his protection. He plundered a
large quantity of grain and other supplies that they
had with them, and put the men to death with cruel
torture. He then sent messengers to all parts of the
Aeduan country and inflamed the people by the same
lies about a massacre of the horsemen and chiefs,
urging them to avenge their wrongs in the same way
as he himself had done.

CHAPTER 39

THE AEDUAN EPOREDORIX, a young
man of the noblest birth and of supreme influence in
his own country, and together with him Viridomarus, a
young man of the same age and influence, but not of
noble birth, had come along with the cavalry in response to a special summons from Caesar. On the
recommendation of Diviciacus, Caesar had raised Viridomarus from a humble position to the highest rank.
These two were rivals for power, and in the recent dispute between the magistrates Eporedorix had supported with all his might the cause of Convictolitavis,
and Viridomarus that of Cotus. When Eporedorix
heard of the design of Litaviccus, he reported the matter about midnight to Caesar. He begged him not to allow the state to fall away from the friendship of the
Roman people through the wicked schemes of some

young men; this he foresaw would happen if so many thousands of men joined the enemy, for their safety could not be ignored by their relatives, and the state could not consider their welfare of slight importance.

CHAPTER 40

THESE WORDS FILLED CAESAR with deep anxiety, because he had always shown special consideration to the state of the Aedui. Without a moment's hesitation he led four light-armed legions and all his cavalry out of camp. There was no time in such an emergency to reduce the size of the camp, since everything seemed to depend on speed; he left the lieutenant Gaius Fabius with two legions to guard the camp. He ordered the brothers of Litaviccus to be arrested, but found that they had fled to the enemy not long before. He urged his soldiers not to mind the hard marching which the critical moment called for; all ranks advanced with the greatest enthusiasm, and after a march of twenty-five miles he caught sight of the Aeduan army. By sending forward the cavalry he checked and hampered their march, and commanded his men not to kill a single person. Eporedorix and Viridomarus, whom the Aedui thought to have been slain, were ordered to move among the cavalry and to speak to their countrymen. When they were recognized and the deceit of Litaviccus was discovered, the Aedui began to stretch out their hands in token of surrender, and, throwing down their arms, to beg for mercy. Litaviccus escaped to Gergovia with his dependents; for according to Gallic custom it is a crime, even in a desperate situation, for dependents to desert their patrons.

CHAPTER 41

CAESAR SENT MESSENGERS to the Aedui to inform them that by his own favor he had spared the lives of those men whom by the rules of war he had a perfect right to put to death; then, having given his army three hours of the night to rest, he started for Gergovia. He had covered about half the distance when some horsemen sent by Fabius came to tell him how critical the situation had been. They reported that the enemy had attacked the camp with their combined forces, fresh troops frequently relieving the tired soldiers and exhausting our men by incessant toil, since on account of the size of the camp they had to remain constantly on the rampart. Many Romans had been wounded by showers of arrows and all sorts of missiles, but the artillery was of great use in resisting the attacks. On the departure of the enemy, Fabius was barricading all the gates except two, adding breastworks to the rampart, and preparing for a similar attack the next day. On receiving this report, by a supreme effort on the part of the soldiers Caesar reached the camp before sunrise.

CHAPTER 42

WHILE THESE ACTIVITIES were going on about Gergovia, the Aedui received the first messages sent by Litaviccus, and wasted no time ascertaining the facts. Some were influenced by greed, others by anger and rashness, an innate quality of the Gallic race, to accept an idle rumor as an assured fact. They plundered the property of Roman citizens, killed some, and dragged others off into slavery. Convicto-litavis helped to precipitate matters and goaded the people to fury, hoping that they would be ashamed to return to their right mind after they had committed a crime. By promising him safe-conduct, they induced the military tribune, Marcus Aristius, who was on his way to join his legion, to leave the town of Cabillonum, and they compelled those who had settled there for the sake of trade to do the same. The moment they started, they attacked them and stripped them of all their baggage. When the Romans resisted, they blockaded them for a day and a night. When many had been killed on both sides, the Aedui called a larger number of men to arms.

CHAPTER 43

MEANWHILE A MESSAGE was brought that all the Aeduan soldiers were in Caesar's power. The leaders hurried to Aristius saying that the state had no hand in what had been done. They ordered an inquiry concerning the plundering of Roman property, confiscated the property of Litaviccus and of his brothers, and sent a deputation to Caesar to offer their excuses. They did this for the purpose of securing the release of their army. But tainted with crime and fascinated by the gain to be derived from the plundered property, as this business involved a large number of persons and they dreaded punishment, they began to make secret preparations for war, and sent envoys to the other states for the purpose of winning them over to their side. Although Caesar understood this very well, nevertheless he addressed their deputies in as kind a manner as possible; he told them that he would not judge them too harshly because of the ignorance and fickleness of the common people, and that he would show the same goodwill towards the Aedui as before. He himself anticipated a greater uprising in Gaul; in order that he might not be surrounded by all the states, he began to plan how he could withdraw from the neighborhood of Gergovia and once more reunite the whole army without making his departure look like a flight occasioned by the fear of revolt.

CHAPTER 44

WHILE CAESAR WAS THINKING about these matters, a chance of success seemed to present itself. When he had come to the smaller camp to inspect the fortifications, he noticed that a hill held by the enemy was left unprotected; on previous days this hill was scarcely visible on account of the large number of the enemy's forces that covered it completely. He was surprised at this circumstance, and inquired the reason for this from the deserters, a large number of whom were flocking to him daily. They all agreed in stating what Caesar himself had already discovered from scouts, that the crest of these heights was almost level, but wooded and narrow where it gave access to the other side of the town. The Gauls, they said, were very anxious for the safety of this ridge; they felt sure that if, after the seizure of one hill by the Romans, they lost the other, they would be almost invested, and cut off from all egress and foraging. Therefore Vercingetorix had called out every man to fortify this hill.

CHAPTER 45

UPON LEARNING THIS, about midnight Caesar sent several squadrons of cavalry to that place with orders to roam about the whole district with more disturbance than usual. At daybreak he ordered a large number of pack horses and mules to be brought out of camp and to be unsaddled; the muleteers were ordered to put on helmets and ride around the hills, presenting the appearance and guise of cavalry. To these he added a few cavalrymen with instructions to range over a wider area for the purpose of attracting attention, and to try to reach the same place by a wider detour. These movements were noticed from the town, which commanded a view of our camp, but at so great a distance it could not be seen what was really going on. Caesar sent one legion along the same height, and when it had advanced a short way, he stationed it on lower ground and concealed it in the woods. The Gauls became more suspicious, and transferred all their forces to that spot to help fortify it. When Caesar saw that the enemy's camp was empty, he ordered the soldiers to cover their crests and hide their standards. He then moved his men from the larger camp to the smaller one in small groups so as not to attract attention from the town. He explained to the commanders of the various legions what he wished to be done, warning them above all to keep their men in check, lest in their eagerness for battle or hope of plunder they advance too far. He pointed out that the disadvantage caused by their inferior position could be remedied only by speed; it was a question of surprise, not of a pitched battle. After these explanations, he gave the signal to advance, and at the same time he sent the Aedui up the hill by another ascent on the right.

CHAPTER 46

FROM THE PLAIN where the ascent began, the distance to the wall of the town was twelve hundred paces in a straight line, if there were no bend in the path. But the distance to be covered was increased by every detour made in order to ease the ascent. About halfway up the hill, in order to check our attack the Gauls had built a six-foot wall of large stones, which followed the long side of the mountain as the contour permitted. They left all the lower part of the slope unoccupied, but covered the upper part of the hill up to the wall of the town with their camps, placed close together. When the signal was given, the Romans quickly reached the fortification, crossed it, and captured three of the camps, and so great was their speed in capturing the camps that Teutomatus, the king of the Nitiobroges, was surprised in his tent, where he was taking a nap. While the Roman soldiers were busy plundering, he barely escaped, with the upper part of his body naked and his horse wounded.

CHAPTER 47

HAVING ACHIEVED his purpose, Caesar gave orders that the recall be sounded, and at once brought to a halt the standards of the Tenth Legion, which was with him. But the soldiers of the other legions did not hear the sound of the trumpet, because a fairly large valley intervened; however, the military tribunes and the lieutenants, following Caesar's orders, did their best to hold them back. But the soldiers, elated by the hope of a speedy victory, by the flight of the enemy, and by their former successes, thought that nothing was too difficult for their valor to achieve, and they did not stop their pursuit until they got close to the wall and the gates of the town. Then shouts were heard from all parts of the city; those who were farther away, alarmed by the sudden uproar, thought that the Romans were inside the gates and rushed out of the town. Matrons threw clothing and silver down from the wall, and learning forward with bared breasts, implored the Romans with outstretched hands to spare them, and not to kill the women and children as they had done at Avaricum. Some were lowered by hand from the wall, and gave themselves up to the soldiers. Lucius Fabius, a centurion of the Eighth Legion, who was reported to have said that day in the hearing of his men that he was spurred on by the prizes offered at Avaricum, and that he would not allow anyone to scale the wall ahead of him, got three men of his company to lift him up, and mounted the wall; then, in turn, taking hold of them one at a time, he pulled them up to the top of the wall.

CHAPTER 48

MEANWHILE THE GAULS, who had assembled, as we stated above, on the other side of the town for the purpose of fortifying it, heard the shouting and were roused to action by many messages that the town was in Roman hands. They sent ahead their cavalry and hastened there with all possible speed. As each man arrived, he took his stand at the foot of the wall and swelled the ranks of fighters. When a large number of them had assembled, the matrons who a moment before had been stretching out their hands to the Romans from the wall began to appeal to their own men, and, in Gallic fashion, to show their hair disheveled and to bring their children forward into view. For the Romans it was an unequal struggle in position and numbers; tired out by the speedy march and the duration of the battle, they could not easily hold out against men who were fresh and unhurt.

CHAPTER 49

WHEN CAESAR SAW that the battle was being fought on unfavorable ground and that the numbers of the enemy were continually increasing, he became anxious for his men. He therefore sent orders to the lieutenant Titus Sextius, whom he had left to guard the smaller camp, to lead his cohorts quickly out of camp, and to station them at the foot of the hill, facing the right flank of the enemy, so that, if he saw our men driven from their position, he might deter the enemy from pursuing them farther. Caesar himself advanced a little with his own legion from the place where he had halted, and awaited the issue of the battle.

CHAPTER 50

BOTH SIDES FOUGHT very fiercely at close quarters, the enemy relying on their position and their superior numbers, our men on their courage. Suddenly the Aedui, whom Caesar had sent up by another route on the right to separate the enemy's forces, appeared on our exposed flank. The similarity of their arms to those of the hostile Gauls alarmed our men greatly; although it was noticed that they had their right shoulders uncovered—the customary sign marking friendly troops—still our troops thought that this had been done by the enemy to trick them. At the same time the centurion Lucius Fabius and those who had climbed with him to the top of the wall were surrounded and killed, and their bodies hurled down from the wall. Marcus Petronius, another centurion of the same legion, tried to break down the gate, but was overwhelmed by a large number of the enemy. Despairing of his own safety (he had already received many wounds) he shouted to the men of his company who had followed him: "Since I cannot save myself and you, I shall provide at least for the lives of you whom by my desire for glory I have brought into this danger. When you are given the chance, look after yourselves." With these words he rushed into the midst of the enemy, killed two of them, and forced the rest a little from the gate. When his men tried to assist him, he said: "You are trying in vain to save me. I have lost too much blood, and my strength fails me. Therefore get away while you have the chance, and get back to your legion." Thus he continued to fight, and a few minutes later fell dead. But he saved his men.

CHAPTER 51

OUR MEN WERE HARD PRESSED on every side, and were forced down from their position with the loss of forty-six centurions. When the Gauls pursued them with considerable violence, they were checked by the Tenth Legion, which had taken up a supporting position on comparatively favorable ground. This legion was in turn supported by the cohorts of the Thirteenth, which had left the small camp and under the command of Titus Sextius had occupied higher ground. As soon as the legions reached the plain, they halted and faced the enemy. Vercingetorix led his men back from the foot of the hill inside the fortifications. On that day our losses amounted to nearly seven hundred.

CHAPTER 52

THE FOLLOWING DAY Caesar called a meeting of the soldiers and reprimanded them for their rashness and their ardent desire for battle. They had decided for themselves, he said, where they should advance or what they should do, had not halted when the signal for retreat was given, and had not obeyed their military tribunes and lieutenants who tried to restrain them. He explained what might be the effect of an unfavorable position, and what he himself had felt at Avaricum, when, although he had caught the enemy without their general and their cavalry, he had given up an assured victory in order that even a trifling loss might not be incurred by fighting on unfavorable ground. As much as he admired the high courage of those men who could not be checked by a fortified camp, a high mountain, and a town protected by a wall, so much more did he condemn their lack of discipline and presumption in thinking that they knew better than their commander-in-chief the likelihood of a victory and the probable outcome of action. "He expected from his soldiers," he said, "discipline and self-restraint no less than valor and high courage."

CHAPTER 53

AT THE END of his speech, Caesar encouraged the soldiers, telling them not to be upset by a reverse which was due to their unfavorable position, and not to the enemy's courage. He was still of the opinion, as he had been before, that he ought to withdraw from Gergovia. He led his legions out of camp and drew them up in battle array on favorable ground. When, however, Vercingetorix refused to come down to level ground, after engaging in a successful cavalry skirmish, Caesar led his army back to camp. After he repeated the same action the next day, he thought that he had done enough to humble the conceit of the Gauls and to restore the spirit of his men, and he therefore moved his camp into the territory of the Aedui. Not even then did the enemy follow; on the third day he reached the river Allier, rebuilt the bridge, and led his army across.

CHAPTER 54

THERE HE WAS GREETED by the Aeduans Viridomarus and Eporedorix, and from them he learned that Litaviccus had gone with all the cavalry to try to win over the Aedui; it was absolutely necessary for them, they said, to get there before he did in order to keep the state loyal. Although Caesar already had many proofs of the treachery of the Aedui, and thought that the departure of Viridomarus and Eporedorix would hasten the revolt of the state, nevertheless he decided not to detain them, so that he might not seem to inflict an injury or give an impression of being afraid. Before they left, he briefly set forth his services to the Aedui—in what humiliating condition he had found them, shut up within their towns, robbed of their fields, stripped of all their wealth, forced to pay tribute and to deliver hostages demanded of them with the greatest insolence; how he had restored them to good fortune and distinction, so that they had not only regained their previous position, but seemed to have surpassed the prestige and power of all previous periods. After reminding them of these facts, he let them go.

CHAPTER 55

NOVIODUNUM WAS A TOWN of the Aedui situated in an advantageous position on the banks of the Loire. Here Caesar had gathered all the hostages from the Gallic states, the stores of grain, the public funds, and a large part of his own baggage and that of his army; here too he had sent a great number of horses purchased in Italy and Spain for use in this war. On reaching this town Eporedorix and Viridomarus learned what was going on in their state: that Litaviccus had been received by the Aedui at Bibracte, a town of supreme importance among them; that the chief magistrate Convictolitavis and a large part of the senate had met with him; and that envoys had been sent officially to Vercingetorix to conclude a treaty of peace and friendship. The two men decided that so great an opportunity should not be neglected. Therefore, they killed the garrison at Noviodunum and the traders who had gathered there, divided the money and the horses and had the hostages of the different states taken to the magistrate at Bibracte. Since they thought that they could not hold the town, they set it on fire to prevent its being of use to the Romans. All the grain they could speedily load on boats they carried away; the rest they burned or threw into the river. They then began to collect forces from the neighboring districts, to post garrisons and pickets on the banks of the Loire, and to display their cavalry everywhere to intimidate the Romans. They hoped that they might be able either to cut them off from their grain supply or to drive them back into the Province under stress of famine. In this hope they were greatly encouraged by the fact that the Loire was so swollen as a result of melting snows that it appeared quite unfordable.

CHAPTER 56

ON LEARNING THIS, Caesar decided that he must act quickly; if some risk should be run in building the bridges, he might be forced to fight the enemy while doing so; therefore it would be better to fight a decisive battle before the enemy collected larger forces at the river. As for altering his plan and retiring to the Province, as some under the influence of fear thought it necessary, Caesar did not think that this should be done; such a step would be disgraceful and shameful; besides, one must think of the difficulty of getting across the Cevennes; and, above all, Caesar was anxious for Labienus, who was separated from him, and also for those legions which he had sent with him. He therefore made very long marches by day and night, and, contrary to everyone's expectations, appeared on the banks of the Loire. The cavalry found a ford good enough for the emergency—the men were able to carry their weapons with arms and shoulders above the water. Caesar posted the cavalry at intervals in the stream to break the force of the current; and, as the enemy was thrown into confusion by the sight of the Roman soldiers, the army was led across the river in safety. In the fields he found some grain and a good supply of cattle, with which he provisioned the army, and then decided to march towards the country of the Senones.

CHAPTER 57

DURING THESE ACTIVITIES in Caesar's camp, Labienus left the raw contingent of recruits recently arrived from Italy at Agedincum to guard the baggage, and set out with four legions for Lutetia, a town of the Parisii situated on an island in the river Seine. When the enemy heard of his approach, large forces assembled from the neighboring states. The supreme command was given to an Aulercan named Camulogenus, who, although enfeebled by age, was nevertheless given this high post on account of his exceptional knowledge of warfare. He noticed a long stretch of marsh which drained into the Seine and made that entire area impassable. Here he encamped, determined to prevent the Roman troops from crossing.

CHAPTER 58

LABIENUS FIRST TRIED to move up sheds, to fill in the marsh with hurdles and earth, and to build a causeway. But finding the task too difficult, he silently left the camp in the third watch, and by the same route by which he had come reached Metlosedum, a town of the Senones situated, like Lutetia, on an island in the Seine. He seized about fifty boats, speedily joined them together and put his men on board. The inhabitants of the town, many of whom had been called up for the war, were so terrified by this strange maneuver that he gained possession of the town without a fight. After repairing the bridge which the enemy had destroyed some days before, Labienus led the army across, and began to march downstream towards Lutetia. The enemy, informed of this by fugitives from Metlosedum, ordered Lutetia to be burned and the bridges leading to that town to be destroyed. They themselves moved from the marsh to the banks of the Seine, and encamped opposite Lutetia facing the camp of Labienus.

CHAPTER 59

BY THIS TIME people were hearing that Caesar had withdrawn from Gergovia, and rumors were spreading about the revolt of the Aedui and the successful Gallic uprising. In conversation with our soldiers the Gauls asserted that Caesar had been prevented from continuing his march and crossing the Loire and had been compelled by the lack of grain to hasten to the Province. When the Bellovaci, who had previously shown signs of disloyalty, heard of the Aeduan rebellion, they began to mass troops and to make open preparations for war. Now that the situation had completely changed, Labienus realized that he must adopt a plan quite different from the one previously chosen. He no longer thought of further gains, or of engaging the enemy in battle, but of bringing the army safely back to Agecincum. For on one side he was threatened by the Bellovaci, who had the greatest reputation for courage in Gaul; on the other, by Camulogenus, who had a well-equipped army ready for action; moreover, the legions were separated from their garrison and baggage at Agedincum by a great river. Confronted suddenly by these great difficulties, he saw that he must rely solely on his own courage.

CHAPTER 60

TOWARDS EVENING he called together his officers. Urging them to carry out his orders carefully and energetically, he assigned each of the boats which he had brought from Metlosedum to a Roman knight, and ordered them to proceed silently four miles downstream at the close of the first watch and to wait for him there. The five cohorts which he considered least capable for action he left to guard the camp, and ordered the remaining five cohorts of the same legion to start upstream with all the baggage at midnight, making as much noise as possible. He also got together a number of small boats; these he sent in the same direction to be rowed with loud splashing of oars. Not long afterwards he himself marched silently out of camp with three legions, and made for the spot where he had ordered the boats to put in.

CHAPTER 61

UPON HIS ARRIVAL there, the enemy's scouts, posted all along the river, were taken by surprise by our men because of a heavy storm which had suddenly sprung up. The infantry and cavalry were quickly sent across under the supervision of the Roman knights who were in charge of that operation. Almost simultaneously, just before dawn, a report reached the enemy that there was an unusual disturbance in the Roman camp, that a large force was marching upstream, that the sound of oars was heard in the same direction, and that a little way downstream soldiers were being carried across in ships. When they heard this, they thought that the legions were crossing at three different places and that all were thrown into great confusion by the revolt of the Aedui and were preparing for flight. Therefore, they too separated their troops into three divisions. A guard was left opposite the Roman camp; a small force was sent towards Metlosedum, to advance as far as the boats had gone; and the rest of their forces were led against Labienus.

CHAPTER 62

BY DAYBREAK all our forces had been carried across, and the enemy's line came into view. Labienus urged his men to remember their former courage and their brilliant successful battles, and to imagine that Caesar, under whose leadership they had often overcome the enemy, was present in person; he then gave the signal for battle. At the first onset on the right wing, where the Seventh Legion was posted, the enemy was driven back and put to flight; on the left, which was held by the Twelfth Legion, although the first ranks of the enemy had fallen, pierced by our missiles, the rest nevertheless put up a stiff resistance, and not a single one of them gave the slightest suspicion of flight. The leader of the enemy, Camulogenus, stood by cheering on his men. The issue was still in doubt. But when the tribunes of the Seventh Legion heard what was happening on the left wing, they led their legion to the rear of the enemy and attacked. Not even then did any one of them yield ground; they were all surrounded and killed. Camulogenus met the same fate. When those Gauls who had been left as a guard opposite the camp of Labienus heard that the battle had begun, they went to the support of their fellow soldiers, and occupied a hill, but they could not withstand the attack of our victorious soldiers. They joined their fleeing comrades; those who could not find shelter in the woods and hills were slain by our cavalry. Having completed this action, Labienus returned to Agedincum, where the baggage of the whole army had been left. Then he rejoined Caesar with all his forces.

CHAPTER 63

WHEN THE REVOLT of the Aedui became known, the gravity of the war spread. The Aedui sent embassies in all directions; as far as they could, they used all their influence, prestige, and money to win over other states to their side. Having come into possession of the hostages whom Caesar had left with them, by executing them they tried to intimidate those who hesitated to join them. They asked Vercingetorix to come to them and to work out a plan of campaign with them. When their request was granted, they demanded that they be given the supreme command. As they could not reach an agreement, a council of all Gaul was summoned at Bibracte. There many delegates from all parts assembled. The matter was put to a vote, and all to a man approved the appointment of Vercingetorix as commander-in-chief. The Remi, Lingones, and Treveri did not attend this meeting; the first two because of their friendship to Rome, the Treveri because they lived too far away and were hard pressed by the Germans. For this reason they held aloof during the whole war and did not send help to either side. The Aedui were greatly distressed at being forced out of their position of leadership; they complained of the change in their fortune, and greatly missed Caesar's favor towards them; nevertheless, having once taken up arms, they did not dare to abandon the other states. Unwillingly, Eporedorix and Viridomarus, young men of the greatest promise, agreed to obey Vercingetorix.

CHAPTER 64

VERCINGETORIX DEMANDED hostages from the other states, and set a day for their delivery; and he ordered the entire cavalry, numbering fifteen thousand, to assemble immediately. He said that he would be content with the infantry which he had used in previous campaigns, and would not tempt fortune or fight a pitched battle. Since he was well provided with cavalry, it would be very easy to prevent the Romans from getting grain and forage. Only, the Gauls must without complaint destroy their crops and burn their buildings, since by this sacrifice of their private property they would acquire lasting dominion and liberty. Having made these arrangements, he ordered the Aedui and the Segusiavi, close neighbors of the Province, to supply ten thousand foot soldiers; to these he added eight hundred horsemen. In command of these he placed the brother of Eporedorix, and ordered him to make war on the Allobroges. In another direction, he sent the Gabali and the nearby cantons of the Arverni against the Helvii; and he also sent the Ruteni and the Cadurci to lay waste the territory of the Volcae Arecomici. At the same time, by secret messages and envoys he tried to rouse the Allobroges, hoping that their anger had not yet subsided after the late war. To their chiefs he promised money, to their state the dominion over the whole Province.

CHAPTER 65

TO MEET THESE CONDITIONS, a force consisting of twenty-two cohorts, raised in the Province by the lieutenant Lucius Caesar, was posted to secure every threatened point. The Helvii on their own initiative joined battle with their neighbors and were defeated; their first magistrate, Gaius Valerius Donnotaurus, son of Caburus, and several others were slain; the Helvii were forced to seek shelter in their fortified towns and behind walls. The Allobroges posted numerous guards at different points along the Rhone and protected their borders with great care and vigilance. Caesar saw that the enemy were superior in cavalry and that, since all the roads were blocked, he could get no reinforcements from the Province or from Italy; he therefore sent across the Rhine into Germany to those states which he had subdued in previous years, and from them obtained horsemen and light infantrymen who were accustomed to fight along with cavalry. On their arrival, because the horses they were using were unsuitable for the coming campaign, he took the horses from the military tribunes and other Roman knights and the veteran volunteers, and distributed them among the Germans.

CHAPTER 66

IN THE MEANTIME, the enemy's forces from the Arverni and the cavalry levied from the whole of Gaul were coming together. A large number of these had already assembled; and while Caesar was marching through the most distant part of the country of the Lingones into that of the Sequani, so as to be able to bring aid more easily to the Province, Vercingetorix established himself in three camps about ten miles from the Romans, summoned his cavalry officers to a council, and stated that the hour of victory had now come. The Romans, he said, were fleeing to the Province and leaving Gaul. This withdrawal would assure the Gauls' liberty for the moment, but little would be gained for peace and security for the future; for after collecting larger forces the Romans would return and continue the war indefinitely. Therefore, he argued, the Gauls must attack them on the march while they were encumbered with their baggage. If the Roman infantry should halt to come to the rescue of the cavalry, they could not continue their march; but if, as he felt sure was more likely to happen, they should abandon the baggage and should try to look out for their own safety, they would lose their essential supplies and prestige. As for the Roman cavalry, they themselves ought to have no doubt that not a man of them would dare to leave the column. That they might make the attack with more spirit, he would draw up all his forces in front of the camps and strike terror into the enemy. The cavalrymen shouted that they should all bind themselves with a most solemn oath not to allow anyone who had not ridden twice through the enemy's column to enter his home again or to approach his children, parents, or wife.

CHAPTER 67

THE PROPOSAL WAS APPROVED, and all took the oath. Next day their cavalry was divided into three sections, two of which made a demonstration on the two flanks of the Roman column, and the third began to hinder the march of our vanguard. Upon receiving word of this, Caesar also divided his cavalry into three sections and ordered them to advance against the enemy. The battle raged simultaneously in all quarters. Our column halted, and the baggage was placed inside the hollow square formed by the legions. Wherever our cavalry seemed to be in difficulty or too hard pressed, Caesar would order that an advance be made and a line of battle be formed. This maneuver hindered the enemy's pursuit and encouraged the cavalry by the hope of support. At length the German cavalry on the right flank gained the top of a height, dislodged the enemy, drove them in flight as far as the river where Vercingetorix was stationed with his infantry and slew many of them. When the other Gallic cavalry noticed this, fearing that they might be surrounded, they fled. There was slaughter all over the field. Three Aedui of the highest rank were taken prisoner and brought to Caesar: Cotus, a cavalry commander, who had quarreled with Convictolitavis at the last election; Cavarillus, who after the revolt of Litaviccus had been in charge of the Aeduan infantry; and Eporedorix, under whose leadership before Caesar's arrival in Gaul the Aedui had engaged in war with the Sequani.

CHAPTER 68

AFTER ALL HIS CAVALRY had been routed, Vercingetorix withdrew his forces from their position in front of the camps and immediately began the march to Alesia, a town of the Mandubii; he gave orders for the baggage to be moved speedily out of camp and to be brought after him. Caesar removed his baggage to the nearest hill and left two legions to guard it. He then pursued the enemy as long as daylight allowed and killed about three thousand of their rearguard. On the next day he pitched camp near Alesia. He reconnoitred the position of the town, and as the enemy were terrified by the defeat of their cavalry, the branch of their army on which they placed the greatest reliance, he exhorted the soldiers to exert themselves to the utmost, and began the encirclement.

CHAPTER 69

THE TOWN OF ALESIA was situated on top of a very high hill, so that it was evident that it could be reduced only by blockade. The foot of this hill on two separate sides was washed by two rivers. Before the town a plain extended for about three miles; on all other sides the town was surrounded by hills, at a moderate distance from the height of Alesia, and having a like elevation. Below the wall, that side of the hill which faced east was entirely occupied by the forces of the Gauls, who had fortified their position with a ditch and a wall of loose stones six feet high. The circumference of the line of encirclement which the Romans were starting to build extended for eleven miles. Camps had been constructed in convenient positions, and twenty-three redoubts had been constructed there. In these redoubts outposts were posted in the daytime to prevent a surprise attack; at night they were guarded by strong garrisons of men in bivouac.

CHAPTER 70

DURING THE CONSTRUCTION of the siege-works a cavalry battle took place in the plain which, as we have noted above, lay between the hills and extended three miles in length. Both sides fought with their utmost strength. When our men were hard pressed, Caesar sent the Germans to their assistance and drew up the legions in front of their respec-

tive camps to prevent any sudden attack by the enemy's infantry. The support of the legions increased the
courage of our men. The enemy were routed, and their
flight was impeded by their own numbers, and they
were jammed together in the too narrow gate open-
ings in the wall. The Germans pursued them vigorously right up to the fortifications. There followed a
great slaughter; some of the enemy dismounted and
tried to cross the ditch and climb the wall. Caesar ordered the legions which were posted in front of their
ramparts to advance a short distance. The Gauls inside the fortifications were as frightened as the rest;
believing that the Romans were coming to attack them
at once, they shouted a call to arms; some in their terror
burst into the town. Vercingetorix ordered the gates of
the town to be shut, so that the camp should not be
deserted. After killing many Gauls and seizing a number of horses the Germans retired.

CHAPTER 71

VERCINGETORIX NOW DECIDED to send
away all his cavalry by night before the entrenchments
could be completed by the Romans. When they were
leaving, he commanded them to proceed to their respective states and press into service all the men who by
reason of age were capable of bearing arms. He reminded them of all he had done for them and urged
them to think of his safety and not to surrender to the
cruel vengeance of the enemy one who had rendered
most excellent service in behalf of their common liberty. He added that if they proved remiss, eighty thou-

sand picked men would perish with him. He told them
that, according to his calculations, he had barely
enough grain to last for thirty days, but that by reduc-
ing the rations he could hold out a little longer.
After he had given these instructions, he sent away the
cavalry in silence in the second watch, through places
where there was a break in our line of works. He ordered all the grain to be brought to his headquarters;
he decreed capital punishment for those who failed to
obey his order; the large herds of cattle, which had
been rounded up by the Mandubii, were distributed to
each man individually; he proceeded to measure out the
grain a little at a time. All the forces stationed outside
the town were taken inside. In this way Vercingetorix
prepared to continue the war until the arrival of reinforcements from Gaul.

CHAPTER 72

ON BEING INFORMED of this by desert-
ers and prisoners, Caesar started the construction of
the following types of siege works. He dug a trench
twenty feet wide with perpendicular sides, so that the
bottom was as broad as the distance between the edges
at the top. He built the rest of the siege works four
hundred feet from this trench; for, since so large an
area was of necessity included, and the entire extent of
the works could not easily be manned with soldiers, it
was important to prevent the enemy from making a
sudden attack by night upon the fortifications, or from
hurling missiles in the daytime at our men when they
were at work. At this distance Caesar dug two trenches,

fifteen feet wide and of the same depth; he filled the inner one, on the level and low ground of the plain, with water diverted from the river. Behind the trenches he constructed a rampart and palisade twelve feet high; to this rampart he added a breastwork and battlements, with large forked branches projecting at a point where it joined the rampart so as to check the enemy's ascent. Towers were erected at intervals of eighty feet along the entire circuit of fortifications.

CHAPTER 73

IT WAS NECESSARY at the same time to get timber and grain and to construct the extensive fortifications; as the foragers had to go long distances from the camp, our forces were consequently reduced in number. Moreover, sometimes the Gauls tried to attack our works by making furious sorties through several gates from the town. Caesar therefore thought that an addition ought to be made to these works, in order that they could be defended by a smaller number of men. Accordingly, trunks of trees or very strong branches were cut, and their tops were stripped of bark and sharpened at the end; next, continuous trenches five feet deep were dug. Into these the stocks were sunk and fastened down at the bottom so that they could not be pulled up, while only the branches were left projecting. There were five rows of these trunks in each trench, joined and interwoven with one another, and anyone who tried to get through them was likely to impale himself on the very sharp points. These the soldiers called "boundary posts." In front of these, in diagonal rows arranged to form a quincunx, pits three feet deep were dug, sloping gradually towards the bottom. In these were sunk smooth logs as thick as a man's thigh, sharpened at the top and hardened by fire, so as to project no more than three inches above ground. At the same time, to make them stronger and firmer, earth was thrown into the pits and trodden down to a depth of one foot from the bottom, and the rest of the pit was covered with twigs and brushwood to hide the trap. Eight rows of this kind were made, three feet apart. The soldiers nicknamed them "lilies" from their resemblance to that flower. In front of these blocks of wood a foot long with iron hooks set in were wholly buried in the ground. These were planted at moderate distances all over the field. These blocks the soldiers called "goads."

CHAPTER 74

WHEN THESE FORTIFICATIONS had been completed, to meet an attack from outside, Caesar built corresponding fortifications of the same kind, facing in the opposite direction following a course over the most level ground that the nature of the country afforded. This line of fortifications had a circuit of fourteen miles. Its purpose was to protect the garrisons of the fortifications from being completely surrounded by a force of the enemy irrespective of its size. And in order to avoid the danger of having to leave the camp, he ordered all his men to provide themselves with a month's supply of fodder and grain.

CHAPTER 75

DURING THESE OPERATIONS about Alesia, the Gauls summoned a council of their leaders and decided not to call into service, as Vercingetorix had proposed, all who were able to bear arms, but to levy a specified number of men upon each state. They feared that in so vast an army massed together they would be unable to control the different contingents, or to keep them separate, or to make systematic provision for supplies of grain. They levied upon the Aedui and their dependent states, the Segusiavi, Ambivareti, and the Aulerci Brannovices, thirty-five thousand men; an equal number upon the Arverni together with the Eleuteti, Cadurci, Gabali, and Velavii, who are regularly under the command of the Arverni; upon the Sequani, Senones, Bituriges, Santoni, Ruteni, and Carnutes twelve thousand each; upon the Bellovaci ten thousand, and as many upon the Lemovices; eight thousand each upon the Pictones, Turoni, Parisii, and Helvetii; six thousand each upon the Andes, Ambiani, Mediomatreci, Petrocorii, Nervii, Morini, and Nitiobriges; five thousand upon the Aulerci Cenomani; just as many upon the Atrebates; four thousand upon the Veliocassi; three thousand upon the Aulerci Eburovices; two thousand each upon the Rauraci and Boii; thirty thousand upon the states which border on the Ocean, commonly called by them Aremorici; to this number belong the Coriosolites, Redones, Ambibarii, Caletes, Osismi, Veneti, Lexovii, and Venelli. Of these the Bellovaci did not furnish their proper contingent, because they said that they intended to wage war with the Romans on their own account and in their own way, and would not submit to the orders of anyone else. However, at the request of Commius, with whom they had some ties of friendship, they sent two thousand men along with the rest.

CHAPTER 76

AS MENTIONED PREVIOUSLY, Commius had rendered loyal and useful service to Caesar in former years in Britain, and in return for his services Caesar had ordered that his state should be immune from taxation and have its rights and laws restored, and had made the Morini tributary to him. But now all the Gallic states were so unanimous in their determination to recover their liberty and their former military reputation that they were not influenced by favors or recollections of friendship, and all devoted themselves with all their heart and strength to the prosecution of the war. When eight thousand cavalry and about two hundred and fifty thousand foot soldiers had been assembled, these were reviewed and counted in the country of the Aedui, and officers were appointed. The chief command was entrusted to the Atrebatian Commius, the Aeduans Viridomarus and Eporedorix, and the Arvernian Vercassivellaunus, a cousin of Vercingetorix. To these were attached men chosen from the various states by whose counsel the war was to be conducted. They all started for Alesia in high spirits and full of confidence; no one of them thought that the Romans could withstand the mere sight of so vast an army, especially as there would be fighting on two

fronts, with those who would make a sally from within
the town, and on the outer side with so vast an army of
cavalry and infantry that came into view.

CHAPTER 77

HOWEVER, WHEN THE DAY on which
they had expected relief had passed and their food supplies had been used up, and they did not know what
was going on among the Aedui, the Gauls besieged in
Alesia called a council to discuss the outcome of their
fortunes. Various opinions were put forward; some
were for surrender, others for trying to break out while
they still had the strength; but the speech of Critognatus
should not, I think, be passed over, for its extraordinary
and atrocious cruelty. He was a noble Arvernian and
considered to have great influence. He spoke as follows: "I do not intend to say a word about the opinion
of those who apply the term 'surrender' to a most
shameful slavery; in my opinion they ought not to
be regarded as citizens or admitted to the council. Let
me concern myself only with those who advocate a
sortie; in their advice, as you all agree, is seen to linger
the memory of our courage of old. But to be unable to
endure privation for a little while is a sign of weakness,
not of courage. It is easier to find men who voluntarily
risk death than men who will bear suffering patiently.
Even so, I would approve the view of those who are in
favor of a sortie (so much weight does their standing
carry with me) if I saw that it involved nothing else
but the loss of our own lives. But in making our decision, we must consider the whole of Gaul, all of

whose people we have summoned to our aid. What, do you suppose, will be the feelings of our relatives and kinsmen, when eighty thousand men are killed in one spot, if they are forced to fight almost over their corpses? Do not rob of your support those men who for your preservation have disregarded their own peril; and do not by your folly and rashness, or by lack of resolution, ruin all Gaul and subject it to everlasting slavery. Because they have not come on the appointed day, do you doubt their loyalty and resolution? Do you think that the Romans are working daily on those outer fortifications simply for their own amusement? If you cannot be reassured by messages from without, since every approach is blocked, use the Romans as witnesses that reinforcements are coming soon; thoroughly frightened by this very thing, the Romans keep hard at work day and night. What, then, is my advice? We should do what our ancestors did in their struggle with the Cimbri and Teutoni, a much less serious war than this one. When they were shut up in their towns, and were reduced like us to straits, they did not surrender to the enemy, but sustained life by eating the flesh of those who by reason of their youth or old age could not fight. And even if we had no precedent for such a course, I should judge that for the sake of our liberty it would be a most noble thing to establish such a precedent and hand it down to our descendants. For what resemblance had that war to the present one? Although the Cimbri devastated Gaul and did her great harm, yet they eventually departed from our country and sought other countries, leaving us in possession of our rights, laws, lands, and liberty. But the Romans have a very different purpose. What else do they seek or desire than, influenced by envy, to settle in the lands and states of those whom they have found to be notable in reputation and powerful in war, and to fasten upon them the yoke of slavery forever? They have never waged wars on any other principle. And if you do not know what is happening among distant peoples, look at the neighboring part of Gaul, reduced to a Roman province, its rights and laws changed, subject to Roman rule, and oppressed by perpetual slavery!"

CHAPTER 78

AFTER THE EXPRESSION of the different opinions it was decided to send out of the town those who by reason of physical condition or age were unable to bear arms, and to try every expedient before resorting to the proposal of Critognatus; however, if they were compelled by circumstances and the reinforcements were delayed much longer, they would adopt that proposal rather than submit to terms of surrender or peace. The Mandubii, who had received them into Alesia, were forced to leave with their wives and children. When they reached the Roman fortifications, they begged the soldiers with tears and piteous appeals to receive them as slaves and relieve their hunger. But Caesar posted guards on the rampart with orders to refuse them admission.

CHAPTER 79

MEANWHILE COMMIUS and the other commanders to whom the chief command had been entrusted reached the neighborhood of Alesia with all their forces, and, seizing a hill outside the Roman lines, encamped not more than a mile from our fortifications. Next day they brought their cavalry out of camp and occupied all the plain, which, as we mentioned above, was three miles long; their infantry they withdrew a short distance from the spot, and posted them on some rising ground. From Alesia there was a view all over the plain. At the sight of these reinforcements, the besieged, filled with joy, rushed together, congratulating one another on their impending deliverance. They then brought out their forces and halted in front of the town; they filled the nearest trench with hurdles and earth, and prepared for a sortie and for every emergency.

CHAPTER 80

CAESAR STATIONED THE WHOLE of his infantry along the two lines of the fortifications, so that in case of need every man could know his post and hold it. He then ordered the cavalry to ride out of camp and to attack the enemy. From all the camps which occupied the surrounding heights there was a full view of the field, and all the soldiers were intently watching the result of the engagement. The Gauls had placed archers and light-armed foot soldiers here and there

among the cavalry to give them support if they had to
fall back, and to check the attack of our cavalry. Many
of our cavalry, wounded unexpectedly by the Gallic
troops, were forced to withdraw from the battle. When
the Gauls felt confident that their men were winning
the battle, and saw our men hard pressed by their
overwhelming numbers, with shouts and yells on every
side, both the besieged and those who had come to their
assistance began to encourage their men. As the engagement was taking place in full view of everyone,
and no deed, brave or cowardly, could pass unnoticed,
both sides were spurred on by desire for glory and fear
of disgrace. Fighting had been going on, with victory
in doubt, from midday to almost sunset; then the Germans massed their squadrons at one point of the field,
attacked the enemy and routed them; when the enemy's cavalry had been put to flight, the archers were
surrounded and killed. Likewise, from other points of
the field, our cavalry pursued the fleeing enemy right
up to their camp, giving them no chance to rally. The
Gauls who had come out from Alesia went back into
the town, in sadness and almost despairing of victory.

CHAPTER 81

AFTER AN INTERVAL of one day, during
which they prepared a great quantity of hurdles, ladders, and grappling hooks, the Gauls left camp silently at midnight and advanced towards our fortifications in the plain. Suddenly raising a shout, that by
this signal they might inform the besieged in the town
of their approach, they began to throw hurdles into

the trenches, to dislodge our men from the rampart with slings, arrows, and stones, and to employ every other method of assault. At the same time, when Vercingetorix heard the shout, he sounded the trumpet and led his men out of the town. Our troops, as on previous days, moved up to their previously assigned stations at the fortifications; with slings, weighing a pound, stakes piled at intervals along the rampart, and leaden bullets they drove back the Gauls. The darkness made it impossible to see far, and many wounds were received on both sides. Many missiles were discharged by the artillery. But the lieutenants Marcus Antonius and Gaius Trebonius, to whom had been assigned the defence of this sector, brought up men from the more distant redoubts, and sent them to the assistance of our men wherever they saw them hard pressed.

CHAPTER 82

AS LONG AS THE GAULS were some distance from our defences, they gained some advantage from the large quantity of their javelins; but when they came nearer, they were pierced unawares by the goads, or stumbled into the pits and were impaled; others were killed, transfixed by wall pikes discharged from the rampart and the towers. Many of them were wounded, but failed to penetrate any of our defences. When dawn came, fearing that they might be surrounded on their exposed flank by a sortie from the Roman camps on higher ground, they retired to their lines. Meanwhile, the besieged brought out the implements which had been prepared by Vercingetorix for a sortie, and filled up the first trenches; but they lost much time in the execution of this task, and before they reached the Roman fortifications, they learned that their men had withdrawn. So they returned to the town without accomplishing their purpose.

CHAPTER 83

TWICE REPULSED with great loss, the Gauls took counsel what to do. They called in men who knew the ground, and from them they learned the positions of the upper camps and their defences. On the north of Alesia there was a hill which because of its huge circumference our men had been unable to include within their siege works; accordingly, they were compelled to place the camp on a gentle slope, on ground which was hardly favorable to us. This camp was held by the lieutenants Gaius Antistius Reginus and Gaius Caninius Rebilus with two legions. After reconnoitering the ground by scouts, the commanders of the enemy selected from their whole force sixty thousand men belonging to the states which had the greatest reputation for courage; they secretly decided what plan to adopt and the best way to carry it out; they fixed midday as the hour of attack. In command of these forces they placed the Arvernian Vercassivellaunus, one of the four commanders, a relative of Vercingetorix. He left camp in the first watch and almost completed his march before daybreak; he concealed himself behind a hill and ordered his soldiers to rest after their night's work. When midday, the hour set for the attack, was approaching, he marched towards the camp mentioned above; at the same time the Gallic cavalry began to advance towards the Roman fortifications in the plain, and the rest of the forces to make a demonstration before their own camp.

CHAPTER 84

WHEN, FROM THE CITADEL of Alesia, Vercingetorix saw his people, he set out from the town; he brought out the hurdles, poles, sheds, grappling hooks, and all the other equipment which he had prepared for the sortie. There was simultaneous fighting on all sides, and the Gauls tried every expedient; they rushed to that section of the defences which seemed weakest. Since the Roman army was strung out over so extensive lines, they could not easily meet the enemy at several points simultaneously. The shouts which were raised at the rear of the combatants had a great tendency to scare our men, because they saw that their own safety from danger depended on the courage of others; for generally what is invisible affects men's minds the most.

CHAPTER 85

CAESAR FOUND a good observation point from which he could see what was going on in every part of the field; he sent assistance to his men when they were hard pressed. Both sides realized that this was the time, above all others, for a supreme final ef-

fort. The Gauls knew that unless they broke through
the lines, they would lose the battle; the Romans, on
the other hand, looked forward to an end of all their
labors, if they could hold their ground. The fighting
was most bitter at the upper fortifications, where, as
we have mentioned, Vercassivellaunus had been sent.
The unfavorable downward slope of the ground
proved a serious handicap to us. Some of the enemy
hurled missiles, while others formed a turtle-shell roof
and advanced; fresh men in turn relieved those who
were tired. Earth thrown by all of them on the fortifications enabled the Gauls to climb the rampart and
at the same time covered up the traps which the Romans had concealed in the ground; soon our men
lacked both arms and strength.

CHAPTER 86

WHEN CAESAR SAW THIS, he sent Labie-
nus with six cohorts to the relief of the hard pressed
men; he commanded him, if he could not hold his
ground, to withdraw the cohorts from the engagement
and make a sortie; but he must not do this unless it was
absolutely necessary. He himself went up to the other
divisions, and urged them not to give way to the strain,
telling them that on that day and hour depended the
fruits of all their previous battles. The Gallic army in
Alesia, despairing of breaking through the Roman defences in the plain because of their size, attempted to
scale the steep slopes; they therefore brought there the
equipment they had prepared for the assault. With a
hail of missiles they dislodged our men who were fight-

ing from the towers, filled up the trenches with earth and hurdles, and tore down the rampart and breastwork with their grappling hooks.

CHAPTER 87

CAESAR FIRST SENT YOUNG BRUTUS to the rescue with some cohorts, then the lieutenant Gaius Fabius with other cohorts; finally, as the fight grew fiercer, in person he led up fresh troops to assist his men. After the battle had been renewed and the enemy repulsed, Caesar hastened to the place where he had sent Labienus. He withdrew four cohorts from the nearest redoubt, ordered a part of the cavalry to follow him, and another to ride around the outer fortifications and attack the enemy in the rear. When neither the ramparts nor the trenches could check the assault of the enemy, Labienus collected eleven cohorts which had been withdrawn from the nearest redoubts and which fortunately appeared on the scene and sent messengers to Caesar to tell him what he thought should be done. Caesar hastened to take part in the engagement.

CHAPTER 88

THE ENEMY BECAME AWARE of Caesar's arrival by the color of his cloak, which he customarily wore in action as a distinguishing mark; and when they saw the squadrons of cavalry and the cohorts, which he had ordered to follow him, moving down the slopes which were plainly visible from the heights, they joined battle. Both sides raised a shout, which was taken up by the soldiers on the rampart and along the whole line of fortifications. Our men dropped their javelins and fought with their swords. Suddenly our cavalry appeared at the enemy's rear, and fresh cohorts were drawing near. The Gauls therefore turned and fled, but in their flight they were met by our cavalry. There followed a great slaughter. Sedulius, commander and chief magistrate of the Lemovices, was killed; the Arvernian Vercassivellaunus was captured alive in flight; seventy-four military standards were brought in to Caesar; only a few of that great army got safely back to camp. When the Gauls in the town saw the slaughter and rout of their countrymen, they despaired of safety and withdrew their troops from the fortifications. When the Gauls outside the town heard what had happened, they immediately fled from their camp. And if the Roman forces had not been worn out by frequent supporting movements and the hard work all through the day, the entire army of the enemy could have been annihilated. However, just after midnight cavalry was sent in pursuit and overtook the enemy's rear; a large number of the enemy were taken prisoner or slain; the rest escaped to their different states.

CHAPTER 89

ON THE FOLLOWING DAY Vercingetorix summoned a council, and pointed out that he had undertaken that war not for private ends, but for the sake of national liberty; and since he must yield to fortune, he offered himself to them for either alternative—to placate the Romans by his death, or to surrender him alive. Deputies were sent to Caesar to discuss this matter. He ordered the arms to be surrendered, and their leading men to be brought to him. Caesar seated himself at the fortification in front of the camp; the chiefs were brought out to him there. Vercingetorix was surrendered, and the arms were laid down. Keeping back the Aeduan and Arvernian prisoners to see whether through them he could regain the allegiance of their states, he distributed the rest as booty among the entire army, one Gaul to every man.

CHAPTER 90

WHEN THESE AFFAIRS were settled, Caesar set out for the country of the Aedui and received their submission. Envoys were sent by the Arverni to Caesar; they promised to carry out his orders. He demanded of them a large number of hostages. Thereupon he sent the legions into winter quarters. He restored about twenty thousand prisoners to the Aedui and the Arverni. He ordered Titus Labienus to proceed with two legions and some cavalry to the country of the Sequani, attaching to him Marcus Sempronius Rutilus. He stationed the lieutenants Gaius Fabius and Lucius Minucius Basilus with two legions in the country of the Remi to protect them from injury at the hands of their neighbors, the Bellovaci. He sent Gaius Antistius Reginus into the country of the Ambivareti, Titus Sextius into the country of the Bituriges, and Gaius Caninius Rebilus to the Ruteni, each with one legion.

He stationed Quintus Tullius Cicero and Publius Sulpicius at Cavillonum and Matisco in Aeduan territory near the Arar, to look after the supply of grain. He himself decided to spend the winter at Bibracte. When the dispatches of the campaign were published at Rome, a thanksgiving of twenty days was proclaimed.